```
--[------->++<]>-.---.[-->+++<]>+.----.++[-                                                                   ++++
+.--.---.------------.--[--->+<]>-.+[->+++<                                                                   .-.>
++++++++++..-[->++++<]>-..---.---[->+++<]>                                                                    .[--
-->+<]>+++.++++.[->+++<]>+.+[->++++++<]>+.+[-                                                                 >-.+
++[->+++<]>++.+++++++++.+++++.---------.-[--->+<]>--.+[->+++<]>+.++++++++.[->+++<]>
--.>+++++++++++...[->++++<]>+..++[--->++<]>.---[---->+++<]>++.+++++++++
+.+++++.---------.-[--->+<]>--.+[->+++<]>+.++++++++.--[----->++<]>.-----------.-[-
-->+++<]>-.+++++++++.+[---->+<]>+++.[->+++<]>+.-[->+++<]>.-[--->++<]>--.+.--.+.++
++.-[--->+<]>-.-[--->+<]>++.---[-->+++<]>+.---------.+++++++++++.-.+++
+++++.+[->+++<]>.++++++++.+++++.---------.+++++.-.-------.++++++++++++.
[++>---<]>--.[-->++++++<]>.++.---.--------.++++++++++.+++[->+++<]>++.++++++++++
++..----.+++++.---------.-[--->+<]>--.++[--->++<]>.-----------.+++++++++++++.-----
-.--[--->++<]>--.[->+++<]>++.++++++.--.-[-->+++<]>.-[--->+<]>.-[--->+++<]>-----
---------.----.--[--->+<]>-.+++[->+++<]>.-.-[--->+<]>-.[->+++<]>++.[--->+<]>+++.-
[---->+<]>++.>-[--->+<]>.+[--->+<]>.++++[->+++<]>.-.++++++++++++.-[->++++<]>-.+
+++++[->++<]>+.>----.[------>+++<]>..-------.+++++++++++.++[++>---<]>.++[--->+
+<]>.++++.++++[->++<]>+.[---->+<]>+++.+[->+++<]>.+++++++++++.-.+++++.---
-------.++++++++++.+.-.+[---->+<]>+++.+++++.[->+++<]>.----------.[--->+<]>--.+++++[
->+++<]>.-.--.-[--->+<]>.-[---->+<]>++.+[->+++<]>++.++++.--.+.++++++++++++.[---->
+<]>+++.+++++.[->+++<]>.+.-------.+++++++++++++.+++[->+++<]>++.--[--->++<]>.--
---.+++.+.+[->+++<]>.[---->+<]>+++.[->+++<]>----.++.+[->+++<]>----.++.+.[->++
<]>+.++.-[-->+<]>--.++.++[->+++<].[->+<]----- ------------ --[->++++<]>+.[->++
+<].[--->+<]>---.[---->+<]>+++.-[--->+<]>-.+++++++++++.[---->+<]>+++.-[--->++<]
>-.+++++++++++.+[---->+<]>+++.[->+++<]>+.-[->+++<].+++++++++++.[->+++<]>.-[--->+<]>
++++.+++.---.---------.------.---[->+++<]>+.-[--->+<]>-.+++++++++++.--.+++.--
--.-------.[--->+<]>---.+++[->+++<]>.--[--->+<]>-.++[--->++<]>.-----------.+++++++
+++++.--------.--[---->+<]>--.[->+++<]>++.++++++.--.--[--->++<]>+.----------.+[->+
+<]>.---.-.-[++>-----<]>.[--->++++<]>+.+++++++++.--------.--[--->++<]>.+++++++<]>-
-.------.--[---->+<]>--.+[->++++<]>+.+.[--->+<]>-------.+++[->+++<]>+.+[--->+<]>--
--.----------.-------.+++++++.+++++.-------.-[--->+<]>--.[->+++<]>+.+++++++++++.+.
++.++++.+.[---->+<]>+++.[->+++<]>+.+++++++++++++.[--->+<]>--.-[---->+<]>++.[-->+++
++++<]>.++.--.--------.++++++++++..-[->+++<]>-..---.+++[->+++<]>.--[--->+<]>--.>
++++++++++..-[->++++<]>-..---.+++[->+++<]>.--[--->+<]>--.----.--[--->+<]>-.+.---.-
-------------.[--->+<]>----.+[---->+<]>+++.+++++[->+++<]>.----------.[--->+<]>--.--
-[->++++<]>.-----------.---.--[--->+<]>-.-[---->+<]>.[--->++<]>-.++++++++++++++
+++.-[--->+<]>-.-[--->++<]>--.-------.+++++++++++..>-[--->+<]>-.-[---->+<]>.[----
>+<]>--.---.--[--->+<]>-.-[--->++<]>--.-------.++++++++++++.+.-.------------.--[--
->+<]>---.-------.-[++>---<]>+.+++++[->+++<]>.----------.[--->+<]>--.+[->+++<]>.---
[----->+<]>-.-[-->+++<]>+.++++[->+++<]>.-----.+++++.-----.---.+++++[->+++<]>+.++++
.-[++>---<]>+.++[--->++<].---.----.[--->+<]>--..+[---->+<]>+++.+[---->+<]>+++.
.+++++.-[->++++<]>-.-[--->+<]>-.+++++++++++.-.+[---->+<]>+++.+[->+++<]>++.[--->
+<]>+.----.--.--------------.+++++++++.---------.--[--->++<]>-.---[->++++<]>-.------
-.+++++.+.---.+++.+[->+++<]>+.-[--->+<]>--.+++[->+++<]>.-.-[--->+<]>.---[->++++<]
>+.--.----------.++++++.---.--[--->+<]>--.+++++[->+++<]>.-.---.-[--->+<]>.-[----
>+<]>++.+[->+++<]>++.++++.--.+.+++++++++++++.[---->+<]>+++.----.-------.[
->+++<]>++.--------.+++++++++++++++.---.+++++++.-[++>---<]>+.---------.---[->
++++<]>.-------------.----.--[--->+<]>-.+[->+++<]>.++++++++++++.-------------.+.--[--
->+<]>-.[->+++<]>++.+++.--.++++++++++++.--.------.[----->++<]>++.++[--->++<]
>.+[->+++<]>.[--->+++++<]>++.--.-----.+++.---.+.++++++++++.--------.-[----->+<]
>-.[->+++<]>+.++++++++++++.---------.-[---->+<]>.+[->+++<]>+.+++++.----..++
+.-------.-[---->+<]>-.---------.+++++++++.[----->+<]>+++.++[->+++<]>.+++++++++++.[
-->++++<]>-.[-->+++<]>--.[---->++<]>--.------.-------------.++++++++++++.+++
+++.+[----->+<]>+++.---[->++++<]>.------.[--->+<]>-----.---[->++++<]>.-------.
----.+.+++++++++++++.+.+.+[-->+++<]>++.++++++++++++.----------.[->+++<]>++.++[--
>+++<]>.++++[->++<]>.-[--->+<]>++.++++++.[->+++<]>.---[->+++<]>-.+[->+++<].++++++
++++++.[++>---<]>---.---[->++<]>.------------.++++++++++++.+[---->
<]>+++.---[->++++<]>-.------------.++++.+++.----.---.-------.++++++.+++++++++.++++
+.-[---->+<]>++.-[--->++<]>--.---.+++++++.++++.+++.+[---->+<]>+++.-[--->++<]>-.++
```

-[----->+<]>--.

```
+++.-[->+++++<]>-.+[->+++<]>+.+,.++++++++++.----.-[--->+<]>.-[---->+<]>++.---[->
++++<]>+.--------.----------.+.++++++++++++.+.+[->+++<]>++.++++++++++++.------
----.+++++.+++++.---------.-[--->+<]>--.++[->+++<]>.-[--->+<]>--.--------.---------
.---.++++++++++++.--------.+++++++++.++++++.+[->+++<]>++.++++++++++++.[++>---<]>--
.+[->+++<]>.++++++++++++.-.------------.++.++++++++++++.++++.-.+[--->+<]>+++.-[---
>++<]>-.+++++.-[->+++++<]>.+[->+++<]>.++++++++++++.--.+++.+++++.-.+++[->+++<]>.+
++++++++++.[-->+++++<]>+++.---[->+++++<]>-.+++[->++++<]>+.++++++.----.++++++++++.-
----------.++.[->+++<]>-.>++++++++++.,-[->++++<]>-.,---.[--->+++++<]>--.>--[----->
+<]>-.--.++.[--->+<]>----..++[->+++<]>++.--[--->+<]>---.+++++++.-[----->+<]>++.>-[
--->+<]>-.-[--->+<]>--.,---.++++++.>+++++++++++.,.>-[--->+<]>-.-[--->+<]>--.[--->+
<]>-----.---[->+++++<]>-.+.+[->+++<]>++.--[--->+<]>---.++.[----->+<]>+++.[-->++++++
+<]>.++.---.---------.++++++++++++.+++[->+++<]>++.+++++++++++.----.+++++.---------.
-[--->+<]>--.-[--->++<]>-.+++++.-[->+++++<]>.+[->+++<]>.---[----->+<]>-.+++[->+++
<]>++.+++++++++.----------.+[--->+<]>--.+[--->+<]>-.+[->+++<]>+.+++++++.+++[----->
++<]>.-----------.-[--->++<]>-.+++++++++++.+[--->+<]>.-[->+++<]>+.+[----->+<]>+++.
[->+++<]>+.+++.--[--->+<]>.[------>+<]>.++++++++++.++[->+++<]>++.+.++++++++++++.--
-[--->+<]>.--[--->+++<]>.-----.[--->+<]>-----.[-->+++++++<]>.++.-------------.+
+++++++.[----->++<]>+.--[--->+<]>---.-------------.--[--->+<]>-.---[->++++<]>.-
-----------.---.--[--->+<]>-.++[->+++<]>.++++++++++.---..+++.+++++++++.+[->+++<]>+.
+++++.--------.+[->+++<]>++.>+++++++++++..[->+++++<]>-.---.++[--->++<]>.++++++++++.
.-----.[--->+<]>-.+[--->+<]>-.++++++.+++[->+++<]>.+++++++++++.--.++.--------------.
[--->+<]>---.+++[->+++<]>.+++++++++++.[-->+++++<]>+++.+++++.[->+++<]>.+++.[-->++
+++<]>+++.+[->+++<]>+.+[---->+<]>+++.--.+++.-------.+++.-------.++++++++++++.[++>-
--<]>-.,.--[--->+++<]>--.[->+++<]>+++.[--->+++++<]>--.>--[--->+<]>-.--.++.[--->+<]>
----.++[->+++<]>++.--[--->+<]>---.+++++++.-[----->+<]>++.++[->+++<]>.+++++++++++.++
+.[-->+++++<]>+++.+[->+++<]>++.[--->+<]>+.-[->+++<]>.--.-[--->+<]>-.-.------------
.+++++.--------.-[--->+<]>--.+[->+++<]>.---[----->+<]>-.+++[->+++<]>++.++++++++++.+++
++.---------.-[--->+<]>--.+[->+++<]>+.+++++++++.-[++>---<]>+.+[->+++<]>.+++++++++++++
+.------------.+.[->+++<]>.++[--->++<]>.---[--->+<]>.+++[->+++<]>.+.+++.-------.
--[--->+<]>-.--[--->++<]>+.----------.+++++++.-[----->+<]>+++.+[->+++<]>.--.++++++++
++++++.-[->++++++<]>-.+[->+++<]>.-[--->+<]>----.--------------.----.--[--->+<]>-.++
+[->+++<]>.,-[--->+<]>--.--[->+++++<]>+.++++++++++.++++.-[--->+++<]>+++.++++++
[->+++<]>.++++++++.----------.[----->++<]>.--------------.-[--->++<]>-.++++++++++++.+
[--->+<]>.-[->+++<]>+.+[---->+<]>+++.---[----->++<]>.--------------.--.++++++++++++
+.--..---------.+++++++++.----------.+.-.-[--->+<]>-.--[--->+++<]>.------.[--->+<]>
-----.---[--->+<]>+.--.++++[--->+<]>.--[--->++<]>+.+[->+++<]>++.[--->+<]>.-.[-->+++
<]>+.++++++++++.+.+.----------.+++++.--------.-[--->+<]>--.+++++[->+++<]>.-.-------
--.[--->+<]>----..+[++>---<]>.>+++++++++++..[->++++++<]>.-----.++[--->++<]>.++++++++++
+..[--->+<]>++.>-[--->+<]>--.--[->+++++<]>+.+++++++.--[->++++<]>.+[->+++<]>+.+[--->
+<]>+++.-----------.+.--[--->+<]>-.>-[--->+<]>-.+++++++++++.+++++.++++[->+++<]>.
+.-[--->+<]>--.----------.[++>---<]>--.++[->+++<]>.++++++++++.+++.[-->+++++<]>+++.+
[->+++<]>.,------.---.--.+++++++++.--.+++++.,----.-[--->+<]>.+[--->+<]>.+++++.--
-----.--[--->+<]>---.+++[->+++<]>++.++.+[--->+<]>--.+++[->+++<]>.+++++++++++++.+.
+[---->+<]>+++.[->+++<]>+.++++++++++++++.----------.-[--->+<]>-.---[->+++++<]>.----
--------.---.++++.++++++++++.[-->+++++<]>+++.+[->+++<]>.++++++++++++++.+++.,-------
-----.[--->+<]>----.,---..-.-----------.+++++.-------.-[--->+<]>--.[->+++<]>+
.>-[--->+<]>--.--[->+++++<]>-.++++++.,-[->+++<]>.--[--->++<]>--.[--->+<]>-.+++++++
+++++.++++++++++.++[->+++<]>.[--->+<]>-----.+[++>---<]>.>+++++++++++..[->+++++<]>+.-
----.++[->+++<]>.++++++++++++..++[--->+++<]>+.-[--->+<]>--.+++++++++++..----------.-
[--->+<]>-.-----------.--[--->+<]>--.[-->+<]>+++.>-[--->+<]>.+[->+++<]>+.++++[->+++
<]>.--[--->+<]>+.,--[--->+++<]>--.[--->+<]>+++.>-[--->+<]>.+[->+++<]>+.++++[->+++
<]>.+.-[--->+<]>--.----------.[++>---<]>--.++[->+++<]>.++++++++++.+++.[-->+++++<]>+++.+
[->+++<]>.-----.---.--.++++++++.--.+++++.[--->+<]>---.+++[->+++<]>++.++++++.--
-----.--[--->+<]>---.+++[->+++<]>++.++.+[--->+<]>--.+++[->+++<]>.+++++++++++++.+.
+[---->+<]>+++.[->+++<]>++.+++++++++++++.----------.-[--->+<]>-.---[->+++++<]>.----
--------.---.++++.++++++++++.[-->+++++<]>+++.+[->+++<]>.++++++++++++++.+++.,,
-----.[--->+<]>----.,-.-.-----------.+++++.-------.--[--->+<]>--.[->+++<]>+
.>-[--->+<]>--.--[--->+<]>-.++++++.--[->+++<]>---.--[--->++<]>--.[--->+<]>--.+++++++
+++++.++++++++++.++[->+++<]>.[---->+<]>.++++++.++[--->++<]>.>++++++++++++..[--->++++<]>
--.[--->+<]>+++.++++[--->+<]>.-[--->++++<]>++.++++++++++.,-[->+++<]>.,--[--->+++<]>
--.[--->+<]>+++.++++[--->+<]>+++.-[--->+<]>++.++++++++++.---.+++[--->++<]>+++.-[--->
++<]>-.+++++.-[----->+<]>-.+[->+++<]>++.+,.+++.------.++++++.----.++++++++++.+++++
+.--------.-[--->+<]>.-[--->+<]>+.--.+++++++++++.---------.-[--->+<]>--.[->+
++<]>+.+++++++++++++++.----------.-[--->+<]>-.+[-----<]>+.------------.++++++++++++++
++.-----.++++++++.+++++.---------.-------------.--[--->+<]>-.-------------.+++++
--.--[--->+<]>--.---[--->+<]>.------.++.--[--->++<]>--.[--->+<]>-.++++++[->+++<]
>-.---------.[--->+<]>--.+[-----<]>.--------.+++++++++.++.+++.++++++++.-[----<]>
++.[->+++<]>++.--[----->++<]>.+++.------------..[--->+<]>-.+++++++++.++++++.+[++>---<]>.>++++++++++
+++.--[----->+<]>-.-[--->+<]>+.+++++++++++++.----------.-[--->+<]>-.[--->++++++<]>
.[------->++<]>+.+++++++++++++.----------.----.+++++++++.----------.++.--[->+++<
.[------->++<]>+.--[--->+<]>-.------------.----.+++++++++.-----------.++.--[->+++<
```

`-[----->+<]>-.`

```
]>+..--[-->+++<]>--.[-->+<]>+++.[-->+++++<]>.[--->+<]>++.---.--------.+++++++++++
.+++[->+++<]>++.++++++++++.-----.+++++.--------.-[-->+<]>--.-[--->+++<]>-.+++++.
-[->+++++<]>-.+[->+<]>.---[-----+<]>-.+++[->+++<]>++.++++++++.+++++.--------.-[
--->+<]>--.+[->++++<]>+.++++++++.-[++>---<]>+.---[->++++<]>.+[->+++<]>++.++++++++++
+.-------.[--->+<]>----.+[----->+<]>+++.---[->++++<]>.-----------.++++.--------.--[
--->+<]>-.[->+++<]>+.++++++++++++.----------.-[--->+<]>-.-[-->+<]>-.+++++++++++
.+[----->+<]>+++.+[----->+<]>+.+.+++++.[---->+<]>+++.+[->+++<]>++.+..+++.------.++
++++.----.++++++++++.++++++.[++>---<]>--.------------.[->++++<]>++.[--->+<]>-.-.[--
--->+<]>+++.--[->+++++<]>+.----------.++++++.-[---->+<]>+++.+[->+++<]>.--.++++++++
++++.-[->+++++<]>-.+[->+++<]>++.+++++++++.----.+++++.++++++++++.-[---->+<]>++.-[-
--->++<]>-.+++++++++++.-.+[---->+<]>+++.+[->+++<]>.+++++.-------.+++++++++++..----
---.++++++++++.-------.++.+++++.-------.-[--->+<]>--.+[----->+<]>+.--------------.-
-[--->+<]>-.+.---.--------------.[->++++<]>-.+++++++++.-[--->+<]>.+++++++++++++++
+..-[->++++<]>-.---.[-->+++<]>++.----.++[--->++<]>.+[->+<]>.[->+++<]>--.--[--->
+<]>--.-----------.------.-[--->+<]>---.+[---->+<]>+++.+++++[->+++<]>.----------.[-
--->+<]>--.+[->++<]>.---[-----+<]>-.+++[->+++<]>++.++++++++.+++++.--------.-[--->
+<]>--.+[->++++<]>+.++++++++.>++++++++++.-[->++++<]>-.----.++[->+++<]>.[->+++<]>-
.[--->+<]>---.+[->+++<]>++.++++++++++.+++.-------.-.-[--->+<]>-.++[->++<]>+.-[-----
>+<]>++++.--------.----.------------.+++++++++++++.------------.--[--->+<]>-.----
--------.++++++.-.-[->+++++<]>-.+++++[->+++<]>.----------.[--->+<]>--.---[->+++++<]>
.------------.---.--[->+++<]>-.+[->+++<]>+.+[-->+++<]>.--.+.+++++++++++.[---->+<
]>+++.[--->++++++<]>-.+[--->+<]>.----------.++++++++++++.+++[->+++<]>++.--[--->+<
]>-.-----.+++.+.>++++++++++..+[->++++++<]>.---[-----+<]>-.+++[->+++<]>++.++++++++
+.+++++.--------.-[--->+<]>--.+[->++++<]>+.++++++++.-[++>---<]>+.+[->+++<]>.++++++
++++++.-.+++++.----------.-[--->+<]>--.+[->+++<]>+.+++++.-------.+[-->+++<]>.----------.
[--->+<]>--.---[->++++<]>.-------------.-------.--[--->+<]>-.++[->+++<]>.+++++++++.---
..+++.+++++++++.+[->+++<]>+.+++++.-------.-[--->+<]>--.+[->+++<]>++.++++.--.+.++++
++++++.[--->+<]>+++.+[----->+<]>+.+.-----------.+++++++++++++.+++[->+++<]>++.----<
.--[--->+<]>-.-----.+++.+.+[->+<]>.>+++++++++++..-[->+++++<]>.[--->+<]>++.[->+++<
]>.[--->++<]>--.++[--->++<]>.-[->++++++<]>.[-->+<]>+++.++++++[->++<]>+.[--->+<]>.
++++++++.+[-->+++<]>.[--->+<]>----.+[---->+<]>+++.---[->++++<]>.-------------.---.--
[--->+<]>-.+[->++++<]>.--------.++++++++.++.+++.++++++++.[++>---<]>--.---[->++++<]>.--
---.--.+.++++++++++++.[++>---<]>.>++++++++++.-[->++++<]>-.++[->+++<]>.++[--->++<]>.-
++++++.>.[-->+<]>----.++++[--->++++<]>.-[->+++++<]>.[-->+<]>+++.++++++[->++<]>+.[--->
+<]>.++++++++.+[-->+++<]>.[--->+<]>----.+[---->+<]>+++.---[->++++<]>.-------------.-
--.--[--->+<]>-.+[->++++<]>.--------.++++++++.++.+++.++++++++.[++>---<]>--.--[-->+
++++++.>.[-->+<]>-----.+++++.++++++.+++[->+++<]>.++++++++++++.[-->+++++<]>+++.+++++[
[->+++<]>.-.----------.--[--->+<]>-.+[->+++<]>.++.++++++++..[++>---<]>--.---[->+++++<
]>.-----.[--->+<]>-----.---[-->++++<]>.-------------.---.--[--->+<]>-.++[--->++<]>.
-------.+.-[--->+<]>---.[++>---<]>.>+++++++++++++.-[->++++<]>-.[--->++++<]>.[--->+<
].[-->+<]>.+++++[->+++<]>.-[->++++++<]>.[-->+<]>+++.++++[->+++<]>+.+[->++<]>.
-----------.-[--->+<]>----.---------------.----.--[--->+<]>--.++++[->+++<]>.[--->+<
]>----.+[----->+<]>+++.---[->++++<]>.-------------.---.--[--->+<]>-.--[->++++<]>--.
[--->+<]>-.++++++++++.++++++++.++[->++++<]>.--[--->+<]>-.+[->+++<]>.-[--->+<]>-.
-.[--->+<]>--.---[->++++<]>.-------------.---.--[--->+<]>-.+[->+++<]>.-[--->+<]>-.
---..-------------.++++++++++.++++++.[---->+<]>+++.+[----->+<]>.--------
-.++++++++.++.+++.++++++++.-[---->+<]>++.+[->+++<]>+.++.++++++++..[++>---<]>--.[--->
+<]>++.[--->+<]>+++.-[----->+<]>++.+++++[->+++<]>.-.----------.[--->+<]>--.>++++++++++
+<]>.[--->+++<]>++.[->++++<]>.[-->+<]>---.+++[->+++<]>.-[->++++++<]>.[-->+<]>+++.++[
-->++<]>.[--->+++<]>-.--.-[--->+<]>----.----------------.-----.--[--->+<]>--.++++[->+++
<]>.[->+++<]>----.+[----->+<]>+++.---[->++++<]>.-------------.----.--[--->+<]>-.
+[->+++<]>.-[->++++<]>-.---.-------.-------------.++++++++++.++++++.+[->+++<]>.++[->++
+<]>.--------.+++++++.++.+++.++++++++.-[---->+<]>++.+[->+++<]>.++.++++++++..[--->+
<]>+++.-[->++++<]>+.+[----->+<]>+++.---.--[->++++<]>--.-[->+++<]>-.++++++++++++.++++++++++
<]>+++.-[->+++<]>+.+[---->+<]>+++.--[->++++<]>--.-[->+++<]>-.+++++++++++.+++++++++
                              -[----->+<]>.
```

```
.++[->+++<]>.--[--->+<]>-.-[--->++<]>-.++++++++++.+[---->+<]>+++.+++++++++++..-[->
+++<]>-.---[->+++<]>.+++++++++++++.---.[->+++++<]>-..++.-------------.-[--->++<]>.
++++++++++.---------.+++.[------->++<]>.++[->+++<]>.+++++++++.+++.+++++.-[->+++<]
>-.--[--->+<]>---.--------------.-[--->+<]>-.---[->++++<]>.-----.[--->+<]>-----.-
--[->++++<]>.------------.---.--[--->+<]>-.+[----->+<]>.-------------.--[--->+<]>-
.++[->+++<]>+.+++++.+.+++++.-------.-[--->+<]>-.---[->+++<]>.+++.[->+++++<]>.+++++
++++.--[->+++<]>+.+.+[->+++<]>++.--[--->+<]>---.++.[---->+<]>+++.+++++[->+++<]>.-
--------.[--->+<]>--.---[->+++++<]>.------------.---.--[--->+<]>-.++[--->++<]>.+++
..+.[++>---<]>+.+++++.>+++++++++.-[->+++++<]>.[--->++++<]>+.[->+++<]>.---.+++.-[-
>+++++++<]>.[-->+<]>+++.++++[->++<]>+.>--[----->+<]>.[--->+<]>--.---[->++++<]>+.-
---------.---.--[--->+<]>-.+[->++++<]>.-[--->+<]>-.---..-------------.++++++++.++
++++.[---->+<]>+++.+[----->+<]>.---------.++++++++.++.+++.+++++++.-[---->+<]>++.+[
->+++<]>.++.++++++++.---[->+++<]>+++.-[---->+<]>.+[--->+<]>+++.--[->+++++<]>--.[->++
+<]>-.++++++++++.++++++++++.++[->+++<]>.--[--->+<]>-.-[--->++<]>.+++++++++.+[--
-->+<]>+++.+++++++++++..+[----->+<]>-.+.+++++.[---->+<]>+++.-[->++++<]>--.---[->++
+<]>.+++++++++++++.---.[->+++++<]>-..++.-------------.-[--->++<]>.+++++++++++.----
----.+++.[------->++<]>.[->++++<]>++.-.++.++++++++.-[--->+<]>+.---[->+++<]>.----
-.[--->+<]>-----.---[->+++++<]>.------------.---.--[--->+<]>-.+[----->+<]>.-------
-----.--[--->+<]>-.++[->+++<]>+.+++++.+.+++++.-------.-[--->+<]>--.[->+++<]>.----
-.+++++.[->+++<]>.++++++++++.+[----->+<]>++.---.-----------.----.----[---->+<]>.
++++++.[----->+<]>+.+[->+++<]>++.+++++++++.----------.-[--->+<]>-.++[---->+<]>.--
-->+<]>.+++.++.+.[++>---<]>+.+++++.>++++++++++.-[->++++++<]>.[---->+++<]>++.[->+++<]>.[--
>+<]>----.++++[->++<]>.-[->++++++<]>.[-->+<]>+++.>-[---->+<]>---.+[----->+++<]>.--
.++.++++.[----->++++<]>.+[->+++<]>.[--->+<]>-----.+[----->+++<]>+++.+++++[->+++<]>.-.--
-------.--[--->+<]>-.+[->+++<]>.+++++.--------.--[--->+<]>---.+++[->+++<]>++.++.-[
--->+<]>--.+++[->+++<]>.++++++++++++.[-->+++++<]>+++.+++++[->+++<]>.----------.[-
-->+<]>--.-[--->++<]>-.+++++.++.+++++.-.[----->+<]>+++.[->+++<]>+.++++++++++++++.--
--------.-[---->+<]>.---[->+++++<]>-.+.-----.+++.-------------.[--->+<]>-.+[---
->+<]>+++.-[--->++<]>.+++++++++++.[----->+<]>+++.-[--->+<]>.++++++.-[->+++++<]>-
.---[->+++++<]>.------------.---.--[--->+<]>-.+[->+++<]>.-[--->+<]>-.---..--------
-----.+++++++++.++++++.[---->+<]>+++.+[----->+<]>.---------.++++++++.++.+++.++++++
+.-[---->+<]>++.+[->+++<]>.++.++++++++..[----->+<]>--------.>++++++++++.-[------>+<]>.
[--->++<]>++.[->+++<]>.[->+<]>--.++[->+++<]>.-[->+++++++<]>.[-->+<]>+++.[-->++++++<
]>-.-[-->+++<]>.-.----.+++++.-.-.+[----->+<]>+++.---[->++++<]>.-------------.---.--
[--->+<]>-.-[->++++<]>--.[->+++<]>-.+++++++++++.++++++++++.++[->+++<]>.--[--->+<]
>-.+++++[->+++<]>.-------------.[--->+<]>--.+[--->+<]>+.+++++++++.-------------.++
++++++++.>++++++++++.++.+++.++++++++.-[---->+<]>++.++++++[->++<]>+.[--->+++<]>.-----
+<]>-.+++[->+++<]>++.+++++++++.+++++.--------.-[--->+<]>--.+[->++++<]>+.+++++++++.++
+++++++.>+++++++++++.++[++>---<]>.++++++++++++..-[->+++++<]>-.----.++++++.[->+++<]>+.>--[----->+<]
>-.+++++++++.++.+++.++++++++.-[----->+<]>++.++++++[->++<]>+.[--->+<]>.------------+.
+++++++.>++++++++++.++[++>---<]>.+[----->+<]>.-[--->+<]>-.++[->+++<]>-.[----->
+<]>-.+++[->+++<]>++.+++++++++.+++++.--------.-[--->+<]>--.+[->++++<]>+.+++++++++.++
+[----->+<]>.------------.[->+++<]>+.+++++++++++++.-[->+++++<]>-.[->+++<]>+.--[-
-->+<]>---..+++[->+++<]>++.+[----->+<]>+++.-[----->+<]>++.+++++[->+++<]>.----------.[
--->+<]>---.---[->++++<]>.--.++.[->+++<]>.++++++[->+++<]>.-.----------.[->++++<]>--.-
[--->+<]>--.[--->+<]>+++.-----.+++[--->+<]>.--[--->+<]>-.+[----->+<]>.---------.++
++++++.++.+++.+++++++.-[----->+<]>++.+[->+++<]>.++.++++++++..++++++++.+[----->+<]>++.-
.-[--->+<]>-.+++++++++.+[----->+++<]>+++.---[->+++++<]>+.--.++++[->+++<]>.-.-[->+++<
]>++.++[--->++<]>.[->+++<]>+.[--->+<]>+.[.[++>---<]>-.+[----->+<]>.--------.+++++++
++.++.+++.+++++++.-[----->+<]>++.+[->+++<]>.++.++++++++..++++++++.+[----->+<]>++.-[->
+++<]>+.--[--->+<]>---.--------------.--[--->+<]>++.---[->++++<]>.-.-[--->+<]>
-.---[->++++<]>.-----.[--->+<]>-----.-[--->++<]>--.---[->++++<]>.+++++++++++++.---
.[->+++++<]>+.-------------.[->+++<]>+.+++++++++++++.----------.-[--->+<]>-.---[->
++++<]>+.-------------.+++++++.+++[->+++<]>.+++++++++++++.++++.+++++.+++[->+++<]>+.-
-[-->++++<]>+++.[-->+++++++<]>.-.------.+++++.++++++.+++[->+++<]>.+++++++++++++.
[-->+++++<]>+++.[-->+++++++<]>.-.------.+++++.++++++.-.+[----->+<]>+++.---[->+++++<
]>.-----.[--->+<]>-----.---[->++++<]>.------------.---.--[--->+<]>-.++[->+++<]>.+
++.++++++++.+.+.[----->+<]>+.+[--->+<]>++.++.++++++..[----->+<]>----.+[----->++<]
]>.[--->+++++<]>>+.++.---.--------.++++++++++++.+++[->+++<]>++.+++++++++++++.
++++++.+[---->+<]>+++.+++++[->+++<]>.+.+.------------.+++++++++++++.+++[->+++<]>++.-
```

```
-[----->+<]>+.
```

```
-[--->+<]>-.+++[->+++<]>.--[--->+<]>-.[->+++<]>++.[--->+<]>+++.-[---->+<]>++.+[--
--->+<]>.-------------.++++++++++++++.------.+++++++.---------.----------.--[
--->+<]>-.------------.+++++.-------.-[--->+<]>--.---[->++++<]>.-------------.---.-
-[--->+<]>-.--[->++++<]>--.[->+++<]>-.++++++++++.+++++++++.++[->+++<]>.[--->+<]>
----.+[---->+<]>+++.+++++[->+++<]>.----------.[--->+<]>--.---[->++++<]>.-----------
--.---.[--->+<]>----.++++[->+++<]>.--[--->+<]>-.+[----->+<]>.--------.++++++++.++
.+++.+++++++.-[---->+<]>++.+[->+++<]>.++.++++++++.++++++++.+[----->+<]>+++.[->+++<]
>+.+++++++++++++.----------.-[--->+<]>-.+[----->+<]>.++.++++++++.[------>+<]>.++++
+.-------.-[--->+<]>--.---[->++++<]>.-------------.++[++>---<]>.>+++++++++++..-[->+
+++<]>-..---.[--->++++<]>.[--->+<]>++.---.---------.+++++++++++.+++[->+++<]>++.+++
++++++++..----.+++++.-------.-[--->+<]>--.>-[--->+<]>---.----[--->+<]>.--------
-.------.[--->+<]>----.>+++++++++++..-[->+++++<]>.[--->+<]>++.+++++++++++..++[-->
+++<]>+.+[--->+<]>+++..---.--------.++++++++++.++++++..-[++>---<]>...--[--->+++<]>-
-.[-->+<]>+++.[->+++<]>+.[---->+<]>+++.[--->+<]>-.-[----->+<]>++.+[->+++<]>.+++++.--
-----.--[--->+<]>---.+++[->+++<]>++.++.-[---->+<]>--.+++[->+++<]>.+++++++++++++++.+.
+[---->+<]>+++.+++++[->+++<]>.+++++.------------.---.+++++++++++.[--->++++++<]>++
+.---[->++++<]>.------------.-------.++++++++++++++.-[->+++++<]>-.---[->+++++<]>.--
-----------.---.--[--->+<]>-.+[->+++<]>++.++++.--.+.++++++++++++.[----->+<]>+++.+++
++[->+++<]>.+.------------.+++++++++++++.+++[->+++<]>++.--[--->+<]>-.-----.+++.+.+
[----->+<]>++++.[->+++<]>+.--[--->+<]>---.-------------.--[--->+<]>--.[--->+<]>-.-
-.+++++++.+.+++.-------------. - -.-[--->+<]>-.[->+++<]>+.-[--->+<]>-.+[----->+<]>+
++.+[->+++<]>.+++++++++++++.--.,--------.+++++++++.++++++.-.+.[++>---<]>.>+++++++++
+.-[->+++++<]>.[--->+<]>++.+++++++++++..-----.-[--->+<]>-.+[--->+<]>.------.+++++++++
++.-----------.----------.+++++++++++.[++>---<]>--.>-[--->+<]>--.[--->+<]>+++.+[->+
++<]>++.--[--->+<]>-.+++[->+++<]>.--[->+++<]>+..--[--->+++<]>-.[--->+<]>+++.[->+++<
]>+.[--->+<]>+..[++>---<]>--.+[----->+<]>.--------.+++++++++.++.+++.+++++++.-[----
>+<]>++.+[->+++<]>.+++.++++++++.+[----->+<]>+++.[->+++<]>+.--[--->+<]>---.-
------------.--[--->+<]>-.-[--->+<]>-.+++++.------.+++++++++++.----------.-----.[-
-->+<]>-----.-[->++++<]>--.---[->+++<]>.+++++++++++++.---.[->+++++<]>+.-----------
--.-[--->+<]>+.+++++++++++++.----------.--[--->+<]>-.---[->++++<]>.------------.---
.--[--->+<]>-.+[----->+<]>.--------.+++++++++.++.+++.+++++++.-[---->+<]>++.[->+++
++++<]>.-.------.+++++.+++++++.-.+[----->+<]>+++.---[->++++<]>.------.[--->+<]>-----.
---[->++++<]>.------------.---.--[--->+<]>-.++[->+++<]>.-.-[->+++++<]>---.
-------.++.++++.+.[---->+<]>+++.+[->+++<]>.++.+++++++.,[-->+<]>-------.>++++++++++
++.-[->+++++<]>.[--->+<]>++.++++++++++..----[->++<]>.+[--->+<]>.,+.[------->+++<]
>.++++++[->+++<]>+.-[--->+<]>--.,--[->+++<]>.++[->+++<]>.+++++.+.++++++.-------.
----[--->+<]>+.,--[--->+<]>--.+++++++++++++.+++.----.-------.[--->+<]>----.+[----->+<]>+
++.[->+++<]>+.+++++++++++++.----------.-[--->+<]>-.++[->+++<]>+.-[----->+<]>++++.-
-------.----.-----------.---------------.--[--->+<]>-.-----------.+++
+++.-.+++++.>+++++++++++.--[->+++++<]>-..,---.+[--->+<]>.[--->+<]>--.--[--->+<]>--.
----------.------.[--->+<]>-.++[->+++<]>+.-[----->+<]>++++.--[->+++<]>-.++++++++++
++.+++.----.-------.>+++++++++++.,--[--->++++<]>...,++.[--->+<]>----.+++[->+++<]>++
.+++++++.+++.----.-------.[----->+<]>--.+[->+++<]>++.+++++++++++++.[--->++++<]>-.
-.-[--->+<]>.+[->+++<]>+.>+++++++++++.--[--->++++<]>...+++++++++..>-[--->+<]>-.[--
-->++++<]>-.+.++++++++++.+[----->+<]>+++.-[--->+<]>-.+++++++++++.+[---->+<]>+++.[
->+++<]>+.-[->+++<]>.++[--->+<]>.+++..+.[------->+++<]>.---[->++++<]>.------------
-.------.--[--->+<]>-.[----->+<]>+++.+.--.-[----->+<]>.------------.-------------.
-.++++++++.--------.+++++++++++.++++++.-.+[----->+<]>+++.---[->++++<]>.-------------.
---.--[--->+<]>-.--[->++++<]>--.[->+++<]>-.+++++++++++.+++++++++.++[->+++<]>.--[-

                        -[----->+<]>++.
```

```
-->+<]>-.+++++[->+++<]>.---------.[--->+<]>--.---[->++++<]>.------------.---.--[-
-->+<]>-.+[->+++<]>.-[--->+<]>-.---..--------------.+++++++++.++++++.[---->+<]>+++
.+[----->+<]>.--------.++++++++.++.+++.+++++++.-[---->+<]>++.+[->++<]>.++.++++++
+..[++>---<]>--.---[->++++<]>+.-------.++++++.------------.+++.[++>---<]>--.-[--->
++<]>-.+++++++++++.[---->+<]>+++.[->+++<]>++.+++.--.++++++++++++.--.---------.[---
>+<]>----.+[----->+<]>+++.-[--->++<]>--.---[->+++<]>.++++++++++++.----.[->+++++<]>
+++.++[--->++<]>.++++[->+++<]>.-[--->+<]>++.++++++++.[->+++<]>.[--->+<]>-.+[->+++<
]>.+++++++++++++.[++>---<]>+.------------.---[->++++<]>-.----------.+++++.-------
----.++.--[--->+<]>-.---[->++++<]>.----------.---.--[--->+<]>-.+[----->+<]>.---
-----.++++++++.++.+++.+++++++.-[---->+<]>++.+[->++<]>.++.++++++++++.[++>---<]>--.-
[--->++<]>-.+++++++++++.+[----->+<]>+++.-[->++++<]>--.---[->++++<]>.++++++++++++++.--
-.[--->+<]>-----.-[--->++<]>-.+++++.-[->+++++<]>-.---[->++++<]>.------------.---.
--[--->+<]>-.---[->++++<]>-.+++++.-.+.+[->+++<]>++.--[--->+<]>-.+++[->+++<]>.-[->+++<]>
.------------.+[----->+<]>+.+.+++++.------------.+.+++++.-------.-[--->+<]>--.-[-
--->++<]>--.-------.-[++>-----<]>..------------.+++++++++.+++++.+[++>---<]>.+++++++
++++..-[->++++<]>-...---.[--->++++<]>.[--->+<]>++.+++[->+++<]>++.++.-[--->+<]>--.
---.+++[->+++<]>++.+++++++++.+++++.-[--->+<]>--.+[->+++<]>+.+++++++++.>+++++++++++
+.[->+++++<]>-....++[->+++<]>+.-[->+<]>.++[->+++<]>+.>+++++++++.--[---->+++++<]>-.
---.+++++++.--[----->+<]>--.+++++.------.+++++++++++.-----------.--------.+++++++++
+.++.+++.+++++++.-[---->+<]>++.+[->+++<]>.++.++++++++..-[--->+<]>+++.-[->+++<]>+.+[-
---->+<]>+++.--[->++++<]>--.[->+++<]>-.+++++++++++.++++++++++.++[->+++<]>.--[--->+<]
>-.-[--->++<]>-.++++++++++.+[---->+<]>+++.+[----->+<]>+.+.+++++.[---->+<]>+++.-[-
>++++<]>--.---[->++++<]>.++++++++++++++.[->+++++<]>+.------------.---.--[--->+<]>--
--.------------.----.--[--->+<]>--.++++[->+++<]>.[--->+<]>----.+[----->+<]>+++.--
-[->+++<]>.------------.---.--[--->+<]>--.[->+++<]>.--[--->+<]>-.+++++++++++.+
++++++++.++[->+++<]>.--[--->+<]>-.+++++[->+++<]>.---------.[--->+<]>--.---[->++++
<]>.-------------.---.--[--->+<]>-.+[->+++<]>.-[--->+<]>-.---..------------.+++++
++++.[---->+<]>+++.+[----->+<]>.++.++++++++..[++>---<]>--.---[->+++++<]>.------.----->+<
]>++.+[->+++<]>.++.+++++++..[++>---<]>--.---[->++++<]>.------.[---->+<]>+++.-----.
[->+++<]>-.-------.>+++++++++.-[->++++++<]>.[--->+++<]>++.[->+++<]>.-----.+++++.-[-
>+++++++<]>.[-->+<]>+++.>-[--->+<]>--.+[----->+++++<]>.+++++.------------.++.--[--->
+<]>--.-[->++++<]>.---.--[--->+<]>-.+[----->+<]>.+++++++++++.------------.++++++++++
.++.+++.+++++++.-[---->+<]>++.+[->+++<]>.++.++++++++..[--->+<]>+++.-[->+++<]>+.+[--
--->+<]>+++.--[->++++<]>--.[->+++<]>-.+++++++++++.++++++++++.++[->+++<]>.--[--->+<]
>-.-[--->++<]>-.++++++++++.+[---->+<]>+++.+[----->+<]>+.+.+++++.[---->+<]>+++.-[-
>++++<]>--.---[->++++<]>.+++++++++++++.[->+++++<]>+.------------.---.--[--->+<]>-.
.------------.---.--[--->+<]>-.++[--->++<]>.+++..+.[------->++<]>.---[->++++<]>-.
+.+[->+++<]>++.--[--->+<]>---.++.-.+[++>---<]>.>+++++++++++.-[->+++++<]>.[--->+<]>
+++.[->+++<]>.---.+++[->+++<]>.-[--->++<]>.[->++++++<]>.[--->+<]>+++.++[->+++<]>.[-->++
+<]>-.--.-[--->+<]>----.------------.-----.--[--->++<]>-.+[-------<]>.-----
---.++++++++.++.+++.+++++++.-[---->+<]>++.+[->+++<]>.++.++++++++..[--->+<]>+++.-[-
>++++<]>+.+[->++++<]>++.--[->++++<]>--.+++++++++++++.++++++++++.++[->+++<]>.--[->++++<
]>.--[--->+<]>-.[->++++<]>++.[--->+<]>+++.-[---->+<]>++.++++++[->+++<]>.-.-
.[->+++<]>-.>++++++++++.-[--->++++<]>.[--->+<]>++.[->+++<]>.---.+++.-[->++++++<]>
.[-->+<]>+++.++++++[->+++<]>.+[--->+<]>.-+.+++.+[----->+<]>+++.---[->++++<]>+.-----
--.[++>---<]>-.+[-------<]>++.++.+++.+++++++.-[---->+<]>++.+[->+++<]>.++.++++++
++..[--->+<]>+++.-[->+++<]>+.+[----->+<]>+++.--[->++++<]>--.[->+++<]>-.+++++++++++
.++++++++.++[->+++<]>.--[--->+<]>-.[->+++<]>++.+++++++++++.-----------.---------.[
--->+<]>-----.+[----->+<]>.-[--->+<]>---.---[->++++<]>.+++++++++++++.---.--------.[
--->+<]>+++.>+++++++++++..-[->+++++<]>-...---.++++++.[->+++<]>+.>--[----->+<]>-.+++++++++.+
+.+++.+++++++.-[----->+<]>++.[->++++++<]>.[--->+<]>-.------.+++++.++++++.+++.[->+++
<]>.+++++++++++++.[--->++++<]>+++.[--->+<]>++.[->+++<]>.+++++++.+[->++++<]>.++
++++++.-------.++++++++++.++++++.[---->+<]>+++.[->+++<]>+.+++++++++++++.---------
-.-[--->+<]>-.++++++[->+++<]>+.-[------>+<]>-.+++++++++++++.-----.+++++++.+++++.--
-------.-----------.--[--->+<]>-.------------.++++++.-.>++++++++++..--[--->++++<]>
...++.[--->+<]>----.++.+++++++.>++++++++++++.[->++++<]>+.,+[--->+<]>..[->++++++<]>
-.-[-->+++<]>-..+[--->++<]>+.>++++++++++.--[--->++++<]>...>+++++++++++..-[-->+++++<
]>.[--->+++<]>++.[->+++<]>.[--->+<]>--....++[--->+<]>.-[->++++++<]>.[--->+<]>+++.
++++++[->+++<]>+.[--->+<]>.+++++.+[->+++<]>.-----.+[----->+<]>+++.---.+++++.[->+
+++<]>.------------.---.--[--->+<]>-.+[----->+<]>.---------.+++++++.++.+++.++++++
+.-[----->+<]>++.[--->++++++<]>.-.-------.+++++.++++++.+++[->+++<]>.+++++++++++++.[
-.-[--->+<]>-.++++++[->+++<]>+.-[------>+<]>-.+++++++++++++.-----.+++++++.+++++.--
------.-----------.--[--->+<]>-.------------.++++++.-.>++++++++++..--[--->++++<]>
...++.[--->+<]>----.+++[->+++<]>++.++++++++++.---------.--[--->++<]>--.-[->++++<]>
>+.++++++++++.>+++++++++++.[->++++++<]>++.....+[--->++<]>+..+[--->+<]>..[->++++++<]>
-.-[-->+++<]>-..+[--->++<]>+.>++++++++++.--[--->++++<]>...>+++++++++++..-[-->+++++<
]>.[--->+++<]>++.[->+++<]>.[--->+<]>--....++[--->+<]>.-[--->++++++<]>.[->+++<]>+++.
++++++[--->+++<]>+.[--->+<]>.+++++++.+[----->+<]>.++++++.------.+++.[----->+<]>+++.++
+++<]>.-------------.---.--[--->+<]>-.+[----->+<]>.--------.+++++++++.++.+++.++++++
+.-[----->+<]>++.--[-->+++++++<]>.-.-------.+++++.++++++.+++[->+++<]>.+++++++++++++.[
```

`-[----->+<]>+++.`

```
-->+++++<]>+++.++[->+++<]>.++++++++++.++++++.---.[-->+++++<]>+++.+[->+++<]>.++.+++
++++..++++++++.+[---->+<]>+++.---[-->++++<]>.-----.[--->+<]>-----.---[->++++<]>.---
----------.---.--[--->+<]>-.---[----->++<]>.---------.---.+.+++++++++++++.[++>---<]>
.>++++++++++++.-[->++++++<]>.[--->+++<]>++.[->++++<]>.[-->+<]>-----..+++++[->++<]>.-[-
>++++++<]>.[-->+<]>+++.++++[->++<]>+.+[--->+<]>.------------.-[--->+<]>----.------
-------.----.--[--->+<]>--.++++[->+++<]>.[--->+<]>++.---[->+++<]>+++.---[->++++<
]>.-------------.---.--[--->+<]>-.--[->++++<]>--.[->+++<]>-.+++++++++++.++++++++.
++[->+++<]>.--[--->+<]>-.+++++[->+++<]>.---------.[--->+<]>--.---[->+++++<]>.-----
-------.---.--[--->+<]>-.++[--->++<]>.-------.+.-[--->+<]>---.[++>---<]>.>+++++++++
>-----.+[->++++<]>.++.+++++++..++++++++.+[---->+<]>+++.---[->++++<]>.-----.[--->+<
--->+<]>++.[-->+++<]>++.----.>++++++++++.-[->++++++<]>.[--->+++<]>++.[->++++<]>.[---
>++<]>----..++++[--->+++<]>.-[->+++++++<]>.[-->+<]>+++.++++++[->++<]>+.[--->+<]>.++
+++++.+[->+++<]>.[--->+<]>----..+[---->+<]>+++.---[-->++++<]>.+++.--------.[--->+<]
>-----.+[->++++<]>.++.+++++++..++++++++.+[---->+<]>+++.---[->++++<]>.-----.[--->+<
]>---.[++>---<]>.>+++++++++++.-[->+++++<]>.[--->+<]>++.[->+++<]>.[-->+<]>-----.+
++++[->++<]>.-[->++++++<]>.[-->+<]>+++.++++[->++<]>+.+[--->+<]>.-----------.-[---
>+<]>----..-------------.----.--[--->+<]>--.++++[->+++<]>.[--->+<]>-----.+[---->+<]
>+++.---[-->++++<]>.-------------.----.--[--->+<]>-.--[->++++<]>--.[->+++<]>-.++++++
+++++.+++++++++.++[->+++<]>.--[--->+<]>-.+++++[->+++<]>.---------.[--->+<]>--.---
[->+++<]>.---------.----.--[--->+<]>-.+[->+++<]>.-[--->+<]>-.---..--------------
-.++++++++++.++++++.[---->+<]>++++.+[->+++<]>.++.+++++++..[++>---<]>--.[->+++<]>++.
[---->+<]>+++.-[----->++<]>++.+++++[->+++<]>.-.---------.[->+++<]>-.>+++++++++++.-[->
+++++<]>.[--->+++<]>++.[->++++<]>.[--->+<]>--..++[--->++<]>.-[->+++++++<]>.[-->+<]>
+++.++++++[->++<]>+.[--->+<]>.++++.[-->+<]>----.+[---->+<]>+++.---[-->++++<]>.---
[->++++<]>.+++.---------.[--->+<]>-----.+[->+++<]>.-----.[--->+<]>++.---[->+++<]>
-.---[-->+++++<]>.-------------.----.--[--->+<]>-.--[->++++<]>--.[->+++<]>-.+++++++
+++++.+++++++++.++[->+++<]>.--[--->+<]>-.+++++[->+++<]>.---------.[--->+<]>--.---
[->+++<]>.---------.----.+.++++++++++++.[++>---<]>.+++++++++++++.-[->+++++<]>.++++
.[--->++<]>++.[->+++<]>.[--->+<]>----..+[---->+<]>+++.---[-->++++<]>.+++.-----.-[--
>+<]>----.--[--->+<]>--.-------------.+++++++++++.++++++.[---->+<]>++++.+[->+++<]
>.++.+++++++..[++>---<]>--.[->+++<]>++.[---->+<]>+++.+++++[->+++<]>.-.[---->+<]>+++.[
->+++<]>+.-[->+++<]>.---[-----<]>.--------------.[--->+<]>-.++.---------.+++
+++++.[++>---<]>--.-------------.---[->++++<]>.-------------.+[----->++<]>..---------
.+[->++++<]>.++.+++++++..[++>---<]>--.+.+++.++++++++..[++>---<]>--.-------------.--
->+<]>----.+[---->+<]>+++.---[->++++<]>.---------.[--->+<]>--.--[--->+<]>-.--[-->++++<]
>--.-------------.[->+++++<]>.-------------.----.--[--->+<]>-.+[->+++<]>.-[--->+<]>-.+++++
+++++.-----------------.++++++++++.+.--[--->+<]>-.+++++[->+++<]>.----------.[--->+<]>--.---[
>.------------.---.--[--->+<]>-.[->+++<]>.[-->+<]>-----..+++++[->++<]>.[->+++<]>.+++
++[->+++<]>.+.------------.++++++++++++.+++[->+++<]>++.--[--->+<]>-.-----.+++.[--
>+++++<]>++.-----.-------.--[++>---<]>-.++[---->+<]>.>---[--->++<]>-.-------------.--
->+<]>.[->++++<]>+.>-[--->++<]>--.--[-->+++<]>.++++++..-[-->++++<]>.+[->+++<]>.
++++++++++++.----------.+.--[--->+<]>-.+++++[->+++<]>.---------.[--->+<]>--.---[
```

```
-[----->+<]>++++.
```

```
->++++<]>.-------------.+.++++++++++.+[---->+<]>+++.+[->+++<]>.+++++.-------.--[--
->+<]>---.+++[->+++<]>++.++.-[--->+<]>--.+++[->+++<]>.++++++++++++++.[-->+++++<]>+
++.-[--->++<]>-.++++++++++.+[---->+<]>+++.---[->++++<]>-.+.-----.+++.-------------
-.-.-[--->+<]>-.-[--->++<]>-.+++++.-[->++++++<]>-.---[->++++<]>.-----------.---.-
-[--->+<]>-.+[->+++<]>.-[--->+<]>-.---..--------------.++++++++++.++++++.[---->+<]>
+++.+[----->+<]>.--------.++++++++.++.+++.+++++++.-[----->+<]>++.+[->+++<]>.++.+++
++++..[-->+<]>--------.>++++++++++.--[->+++++<]>-.++.+++[->+++<]>+.[->+++++<]>++.
+++++++++.---------.++++++++++++++.+++[->+++<]>++.--[--->+<]>-.-----------.+++++.-
------.-[--->+++<]>--.[->+++++<]>-.-[--->++<]>.-.----.+++++.-.>+++++++++++..>-[--->
+<]>.+[--->+<]>+.++++[->+++<]>.--[--->+<]>-.---[->++++<]>.-------------.---.--[--
>+<]>-.[->+++<]>.[-->+<]>--.++[->+++<]>.[->+++<]>.+++++[->+++<]>.+.-----------.+++
+++++++++.+++[->+++<]>++.--[--->+<]>-.-----.+++.[-->+++++<]>+++.---[->++++<]>.--
---.[--->+<]>-----.++++++[-->+++++<]>.++++++.-.-----.+++++.-.[----->+<]>+++.---[->+++++<
]>.-------------.---.--[--->+<]>-.--[->++++<]>--.[->+++<]>.+++++++++++++.+++++++++.
++[->+++<]>.--[--->+<]>-.+++++[->+++<]>.----------.[--->+<]>--.---[->+++++<]>.-----
-------.---.--[--->+<]>-.+[->+++<]>.-[--->+<]>-.---..-------------.++++++++++.++++
++.[----->+<]>++.+[----->+<]>.+++.+++.++++++++.-[----->+<]>++.+.+[->
+++<]>.++.++++++++..[++>---<]>--.[->+++<]>+.--[--->+<]>--.+[---->+<]>+++.[->+++<]>
+.-[->+++<]>.+[->+++<]>.+++++.-------.--[--->+<]>---.+++[->+++<]>++.++.-[--->+<]>
--.+++[->+++<]>.++++++++++++++.++[++>---<]>.>+++++++++++..-[->+++++<]>-.---.++[->++
<]>+.-[----->+<]>++++.--[->+++<]>-.++++++++++++.+++.------..-.+[
---->+<]>+++.+++++.-[->+++<]>.----------.[--->+<]>--.++++[->+++<]>+.+[--->+<]>.++.+++
++.-.[++>---<]>+.+[->+++++++<]>-.-[--->+++<]>.-.----.+++++.-.[---->+<]>+++.[-->+++
++<]>.[--->+<]>+++.---.--------.+++++++++++++.+++[->+++<]>++.++++++++++.++++++.>++
++++++++.-[->+++++<]>-.+[->+++<]>+.+[--->+<]>++.+++++.--------.++++++++++.++++++++.
------.+++++++.----.--------.--[--->+<]>-.+[->+++<]>+.+[--->+++<]>++.-------.--[--->
+<]>---.+++[->+++<]>++.++.-[--->+<]>--.+++[->+++<]>.++++++++++++++.[-->+++++<]>+++
.++++.+[->+++<]>.++.++++++.-.-.+[---->+<]>+++.[->+++++<]>++.++++++++++++.+++++++++++
-----.-[--->+<]>-.[-->+++++<]>-.-[--->++<]>.-.----.+++++.-.>+++++++++++..--[--->++
++<]>...++.[--->+<]>----.+++[->+++<]>++.++++++++++.+++++.--------.-[--->+<]>--.+[->
+++<]>+.+++++++++.>+++++++++++.+[->+++++<]>.++.--.++.--.++.>+++++++++++.--[--->++++<]
>...+++++++++++.-[->+++++<]>.[--->+<]>.[->+++<]>----.++++.------.[--->+<]>---.+[
->++++++<]>.[-->+<]>+++.>-[--->+<]>---.+[----->+<]>.--.++.++++.[->+++++++<]>.+[-
>+++<]>.[--->+<]>----.+[---->+<]>+++.-[--->+<]>-.+++++.++.+++++.-.[++>---<]>.>++
++++++++.-[->++++++<]>.[--->+<]>+++.[-->+++<]>.[->+++<]>--.++[->+++<]>.-[->++++++<]>.
[-->+<]>+++.[--->++++<]>-.-[--->+<]>-.+++++.++.+++++.-.[---->+<]>+++.+[->
+++<]>.+++++.--------.--[--->+<]>---.+++[->+++<]>++.++.-[--->+<]>--.+++[->+++<]>.+
+++++++++++++.[-->+++++<]>+++.+++++++++++.-[--->+<]>---.+++[->++++<]>+.>-[--->+<]>-.[--
-[------>+<]>.-------------.++++++++++.-----------.---.--[--->+<]>-.+++[->++++<]
>.-.-[--->+<]>-.---[->++++<]>.-------------.++++++++++.------------.--[--->+<]>-.
.---[->++++<]>.-----------.++++.--------.--[--->+<]>-.+[++>---<]>.++++++++++++.-
[->+++++<]>-...---.[--->+++++<]>.[--->+<]>++.---.---------.++++++++++++.+++[->++++<]>+
+.++++++++++++.[->+++++<]>-.>-[--->+<]>-.[---->++++<]>-.-------.--[--->+<]>-.[--
-->+<]>+++.[-->+++<]>-.-[-->+++<]>.-.----.+++++.-.-.+[---->+<]>+++.++++[->+++<]>
+.+[--->+<]>.++.++++++.-.[----->+<]>+++.[----->+<]>+++.+++.-[--->+<]>--.+++[->+++<]
+[->+++<]>+.+[->+++++<]>+.>+++++++++++.--[--->++++<]>.++.[--->+<]>----.+++[->+++
<]>++.+++++++++++.+++++.---------.-[--->+<]>--.+[->+++<]>+.++++++++.>++++++++++++.[->++
++++.--.---[->++++<]>.+[->+++<]>++.++.-[--->+<]>--.++[->+++<]>.++[->+++<]>+.--[--->
+<]>--.[-->+++<]>+.-[--->+<]>.++[->+++<]>.[-->+<]>--.[-->+<]>.-.+[->+<]>.[--
------>+<]>.[-->+++<]>.>++++++++++++.--[--->++++<]>...>++++++++++++.--[->+++++<]>.[--
->++[--->++.[->+++<]>.[--->++.[--[->+++++<]>.++++[->+++<]>.-[->+++++<]>.[-->+<]
>+++.++++.+[---->+<]>+.++.++++.-.-.+[---->+<]>+++.---[->++++<]>.-----------.++++++++++++
.-------.--[--->+<]>---.+++[->+++<]>++.++.-[--->+<]>--.+++[->+++<]>.+++++++++++++
.[-->+++++<]>+++.[->+++<]>+.++++++++++++++.----------.-[--->+<]>-.---[->++++<]>.+
.------.+++++++.----.-------.+++++.++.>++++++++++.--[--->++++<]>...+.-----.+++.-


                          +[--------->+<]>-.
```

```
------------.--[--->+<]>-.-[--->++<]>-.+++++.++.+++++.-.[---->+<]>+++.-[--->++<]>
-.+++++.-[->+++++<]>-.---[->+++++<]>.------------.---.--[--->+<]>-.+[----->+<]>+.-
--------.[--->+<]>+.----.[---->+<]>+++.+[->+++<]>.++.++++++++..++++++.+[----->+<]>
+++.[->+++<]>+.--[--->+<]>--.+[----->+<]>+++.++[--->++<]>.+++.-.-------.-[--->+<]>
--.[->+++<]>+.--[--->+<]>--.+[----->+<]>+++.---[->+++++<]>.------------.---.--[--->
+<]>-.-[--->++<]>-.+++++.++.+++++.-.[---->+<]>+++.-[->+++++<]>+.+.+++++.[----->+<]>+
+++++++.---------..[-->+<]>-------.+[->+++<]>.+++++.-------.--[--->+<]>---.+++[->+
++<]>++.++.-[--->+<]>--.+++[->+++<]>.+++++++++++++.[--->+++++<]>+++.++++++++.-[---
>+++++<]>.>-[--->+<]>--.--[--->++<]>-.++++++..-[->++++<]>.+[->+++<]>.++++++++++++
.-----------.+.--[--->+<]>-.[-->+++<]>.-------.+++++.>+++++++++++.-[->+++++<]>.[--
->++<]>++.[->+++<]>.[--->++<]>----.[-->+++<]>+.-[--->++<]>.++[--->+++<]>.+++.-[->+
+++++<]>.[-->+<]>+++.-[->+++++++<]>.[-->+<]>+++.[--->+++++<]>-.-[-->+++<]>.--[->+++<]>.
-.----.+++++.-.+.[---->+<]>+++.---[->++++<]>.------------.---.--[--->+<]>.--[->
++++<]>--.[->+++<]>-.+++++++++++.++++++++++.++[->+++<]>.[--->+<]>----.+[----->+<]>+
++.+++++[->+++<]>.----------.[--->+<]>--.---[->++++<]>.------------.---.--[--->+<]
>-.+[->+++<]>.++.+++++++..+++++++.+[---->+<]>+++.[->+++<]>+.+++++++++++.-------
---.-[--->+<]>-.+[----->+<]>+.++.+++++++.+[->+++<]>+.[--->+<]>+++.---[->++++<]>+++.-
--[----->++<]>.----------.--.+.+++++++++++++.[---->+<]>+++.---[->++++<]>+.-------.+
+++++.-----------.+++.[++>---<]>--.-[--->++<]>-.+++++++++++++.[----->+<]>+++.---[---
-->+++<]>.-------------.----.++.+++++.---.[--->++<]>+.+[----->+<]>+++.+++.-[->+++++<
]>.-------------.---.--[--->+<]>-.[-->+++++<]>--.++++++++.----------..[-->+<]>---
.+[->+++<]>.+++++.-------.--[--->+<]>---.+++[->+++<]>++.++.-[--->+<]>--.+++[->+++
<]>.+++++++++++++.++[++>---<]>.>+++++++++..-[->+++++<]>...>+++++++++++..-[->++++++<
]>-.--.++[-->+++<]>+.-------.++[--->++<]>.[-->+++<]>+.+[----->+<]>.--[---->+<]>.[-
-->+<]>-.+++++++++++++.-----------.++.-.-[--->+<]>-.>-[--->+<]>-.-[----->+++<]>.--.
+++++.+++++++.-----.+++++++++.++++.++[->+++<]>.[--->+<]>-----.>+++++++++++..-[->++++<
]>-..---.+++++++[->+++<]>+.>--[----->+<]>-.++++++++.++.+++.++++++++.-[----->+<]>+++.[-
->+++++<]>-.+[->+++<]>.-------------.+++++++++++++.+++[->+++<]>++.--[--->+<]>-.----
-------.+++++++.-.+++++.+[---->+<]>+++.++++++++.-[->+++<]>-.[--->+<]>.+++++++.[----
--->+<]>.+++++.-------.---[->+++<]>.------------.+[->+++<]>+.+[--->+<]>+++.+.++++++
+++.[->+++<]>+.[--->+<]>.++++++++.[------>+<]>.+++++.-------.--[--->+<]>.>+[--->+<]>
.+++++++++++.++++++++++++.++++++++.++[->+++<]>.[--->+<]>----.>++++++++++..--[---
>++++<]>...++.[--->+<]>----.+++[->+++<]>++.+++++++++.+++++.--------.-[--->+<]>--.+[
->+++<]>+.+++++++++.>++++++++++.+[->+++<]>-....++[->+++<]>+.++[------>+<]>.+[--->+
+<]>+.+[----->+<]>..[----->+++<]>.+[->+++<]>+.+++++++++++.--[--->+++<]>.>+++++++++
+++.--[->+++++<]>.[--->+++<]>++.[->+++<]>.[-->+<]>-----.....+++++[->+++<]>.-[->++++
++<]>.[-->+<]>+++.>-[--->+<]>--.[----->+++<]>.[--->+<]>---.-.+[----->+<]>+++.---[-
>++++<]>.-------------.---.--[--->+<]>-.--[->+++++<]>--.[--->+<]>.+++++++++++++.++++
+++++.++[->+++<]>.--[--->+<]>.+++++.+[->+++<]>.---------.[--->+<]>--.---[->+++++<]>
.------------.---.--[--->+<]>-.++[->+++<]>.+++.+++++++++.+.+.[---->+<]>+++.+[->++
+<]>.++.+++++++..[++>---<]>--.---[->+++<]>.-----.[--->+<]>-----.-----.>+++<]>-.-
-----.>+++++++++.-[->+++<]>.------------.[--->+<]>--.--[--->+<]>-.++[->+++<]>.+[--->
++<]>+.+[----->+<]>..[--->++++<]>.+[->+++<]>+.+++.-[->+++++++<]>.[-->+<]>+++.+++++++
[->++<]>+.[--->+<]>.+++++++.+[->+++<]>.[--->+<]>----.+[----->+<]>+++.---[->++++<]>
.------------.---.--[--->+<]>-.--[->+++++<]>.[--->+<]>-.+++++++++++.+++++++++++.++
[->+++<]>.--[--->+<]>-.---[->+++++<]>.------.[--->+<]>-----.---[->++++<]>.--------
---.---.--[--->+<]>-.---[->+++++<]>.------------.+.++++++++++.--------------.-[--->
+<]>-.+[->+++<]>.++.+++++++..[++>---<]>-.[->+++<]>+.++++++++++++++++.----------.-[-
-->+<]>-.---[----->+<]>.------------.[--->+<]>-.---[->+++++<]>.[--->+<]>---.-
.+[----->+<]>+++.---[->+++++<]>.------------.---.--[--->+<]>-.++[->+++<]>.+++.+++++
++++.+.+.[---->+<]>+++.+[->+++<]>.++.+++++++..[++>---<]>--.---[->+++++<]>.-----.[-
-->+<]>-----.-[->+++++<]>.---.--[--->+<]>.++++++++++++.---.[->+++++<]>+++.>+++++++
+++.-[--->++<]>-.>+[--->+<]>.+++++++++++++.+++++++++++.++++++++++++.++[->+++<]>.[--
->+<]>----..>+++++++++..--[--->++++<]>...++.[--->+<]>----.+++[->+++<]>++.++++++++


                        +[--------->+<]>.
```

```
.+++++.---------.-[--->+<]>--.+[->+++<]>+.++++++++.>++++++++++.+[->++++<]>-.....++
[->++<]>+.++[--->++<]>..+[--->++<]>+.-[-->++++<]>-.+[--->++<]>+.+[----->+<]>.+.[--
-->+++<]>.+[->+++<]>+.[--->++<]>...[-->+++<]>--.-[--->++<]>...[->+++++<]>-.-[--->++
+<]>-...--[----->+++<]>.+[->+++<]>+.>+++++++++.--[--->+++<]>...>++++++++++..-[->+
++++<]>.[--->++<]>++.+[->+++<]>+.+[--->+<]>+++.+.-------.----.[--->+<]>----.+[----
>+<]>+++.---[->++++<]>.------------.---.--[--->+<]>-.--[->++++<]>--.[->++++<]>-.++
++++++++.++++++++.++[->+++<]>.--[--->+<]>-.+++++[->+++<]>.---------.[--->+<]>--
.---[->+++<]>.------------.---.--[--->+<]>-.++[->+++<]>.+++.+++++++++.+.+.[---->
+<]>+++.+[->+++<]>.++.+++++++..[++>---<]>--.---[->++++<]>.-----.[--->+<]>-----.--
-[->++++<]>.-------------.---.--[--->+<]>-.---[->+++<]>.-------------.+.+++++++++.
--------------.-[--->+<]>-.[->+++<]>+.++++++++++++.----------.-[--->+<]>-.++[->+
++<]>.++++++++++.++++++.---.++.-------------.--[--->+<]>--.+[->+++<]>.++.++++++++..+
++++++.+[++>---<]>.>++++++++++.-[--->++<]>.[--->++<]>++.>-[--->++<]>-.[----->++++
<]>-.---.++++++++++.[----->++<]>.-------------.+[----->+<]>.++.++++++++.+[->++++<]>.[
--->+<]>----.+[----->+<]>+++.---[->++++<]>.-------------.---.--[--->+<]>-.--[->+++++
<]>--.[->+++<]>-.++++++++++++.++++++++++.++[->+++<]>.--[--->+<]>-.[->+++<]>++.-.++.
++++++++.-[++>---<]>+.++[->+++<]>.++[--->++<]>.++++++++++++.---.--.[->+++++<]>-.---
-------------.---.--[--->+<]>-.++[->+++<]>.++++++++++.++++++.---.++.--------------
[--->+<]>--.+[->+++<]>.++.++++++++..[++>---<]>--.---[->++++<]>.-----.[--->+<]>----
-.---[->++++<]>.-------------.---.--[--->+<]>-.++[->+++<]>.+++.++++++++++.+.+.[----
>+<]>+++.+[->+++<]>.++.++++++++..[->+++<]>---------.>+++++++++++.-[->+++++<]>-.---.[
->++<]>+.--[----->++<]>-.----------.+++++++++++.-------------.+++++.--------.[--->+<
]>---.------------.------.[--->+<]>-.[->+++++<]>-.+[--->+<]>.------------.++++++++
+++++.+++[->++++<]>++.--[--->+<]>-.------------.++++++.-.++++++.+[----->+<]>+++.+++++
+++.-[->+++++<]>+.[->+++<]>-.+++++.+++++++++++.------------.++++++.-.[----->++
<]>.-------------.>-[--->+<]>--.[--->++<]>+++.+[->+++<]>.[--->++<]>--.--.+++[->++++
<]>++.++.-[--->+<]>--.------------.++++++.-.[----->++<]>.-------------.++++++[->+++<]
>+.+[->+++<]>.----------.++++++++.-----------.+++++.---.---.------.--.--[--->+
<]>-.------------.++++++.-.[----->++<]>.-------------.++[->+++<]>.++[--->++<]>.[->+
++++<]>.[------>+<]>.++++++++++.----------.++++++.-.++[++>---<]>+.>+++++++++++..-[
->+++++<]>-...---.[->+++<]>+.+[--->+++<]>+.+++++.+++++++++++.------------.++++++.-.>
+++++++++++.--[--->+++<]>...++.[--->+<]>----.+++[->+++<]>++.+++++++++++.-----.-----
---.-[--->+<]>--.+[->+++<]>+.++++++++.>+++++++++.+[->++++<]>-.....-[--->+++<]>-.+
[--->+++<]>+...++[->+++<]>+.-[--->+<]>.[->+++++<]>-.-[--->++<]>-.--[----->+++<]>.+[
->+++<]>+.>++++++++++.--[--->+++<]>...>++++++++..-[--->+++<]>.[--->++<]>++.>-[-
--->+<]>-.[----->+++<]>---.-.+[--->+<]>+++.---[->++++<]>.-------------.
---.--[--->+<]>-.++[->+++<]>.+++.++++++++++.+.+.[---->+<]>+++.+[->+++<]>.++.++++++
+..[++>---<]>--.---[->++++<]>.-----.[--->+<]>-----.-----[->+++<]>-.--[--->+<]>--.
[->+++<]>+.+++++++++++++.------------.[--->+<]>-.---[->++++<]>.-------------.---.--
[--->+<]>-.--[->+++++<]>-.++++[->+++<]>.--.+++++++++++.-.-----------------.-[--->+<]>-.
+[->+++<]>.++.++++++++..[++>---<]>--.---[->++++<]>.-----.[--->+<]>-----.++[--->+++<
]>.-----.>+++++++++++.-[->++++++<]>.[--->++<]>++.[->++++<]>.------.-[--->++<]>.[->+++
++<]>-.-[----->++<]>-.--[----->+++<]>.+[->+++<]>+.+++.-[--->++<]>.-----.---<]>+++.[->+
+<]>+.+[--->+++<]>+..--[--->++<]>---.+[----->+<]>+++.---[->++++<]>.-------------.---.
-[--->+<]>-.--[->+++++<]>--.[->+++<]>-.+++++++++++++.++++++++++.++[->+++<]>.--[--->+<
]>-.+++++[->+++<]>.---------.[--->+<]>--.---[->+++<]>.-------------.---.--[--->+<
]>-.++.++++++++..[++>---<]>--.---[->++++<]>.------.-------------.-[--->+<]>-.+[->+
[--->+<]>-.--[->+++++<]>-.++++[->+++<]>.--.+++++++++++.-.-----------------.-[--->+<]>-.
+[->+++<]>.++.++++++++..[++>---<]>--.[->+++<]>+.+++++++++++++.-----.-[--->+<]>-.---[--
-->+++<]>.-------------.---.--[--->+<]>-.---[->+++++<]>-.++++[->+++<]>.--.+++++
++++++.-.-----------.-[--->+<]>.+[->+++<]>.++.++++++++..[++>---<]>--.---[->+++++<]
>.-----.[--->++<]>++.>+++++++++++.-[->++++++<]>.[--->++<]>++.[->++++<]>.------.-[--
-->++<]>.[->+++++<]>-.-[----->++<]>-.--[----->+++<]>.+[->+++<]>+.+++.-[--->++<]>.---
--.---<]>+++.[->++<]>+.+[--->+++<]>+..--[--->++<]>---.+[----->+<]>+++.++++++++++.+[->
+++<]>+.-[--->++<]>.[----->+++<]>.---[->++++<]>-.--[----->+++<]>.+[->+++<]>+.>++++++
+++++.--[--->+++<]>...>+++++++++++..-[->+++++<]>.[--->++<]>++.>-[--->++<]>--.[--->
+<]>++++.+[->+++<]>.[--->++<]>--.--.+++[->++++<]>++.++.-[--->++<]>--.-.+[----->+<]>++
+.->++++++++++.++[->+++<]>.--[--->+<]>.+++++[->+++<]>.---------.[--->+<]>--.---[->
++++<]>.------------.---.--[--->+<]>-.++++[->+++<]>.--.+++++++++++

                                -[----->+<]>--.-.
```

```
+.-.-----------.-[--->+<]>-.+[->+++<]>.++.+++++++..[++>---<]>--.++[->+++<]>.++++++
+++++.---.--.[->+++++<]>-.---[->++++<]>.-------------.----.--[--->+<]>-.++[->+++<]
>.+++.+++++++++.+.+.[---->+<]>+++.+[->+++<]>.++.+++++++..[-->+<]>--------.>++++++
++++..-[->++++<]>-...---.++++++[->+++<]>+.+[-->+++<]>.---------.++++++++.---------
--.+++++++.----.---.------.--.--[--->+<]>-.-----------.++++++.-.>++++++++++.--[-
-->++++<]>...++.[-->+<]>-----.+++[->+++<]>++.+++++++.+++++.-------.-------[-->+<]>-
.+[->+++<]>+.+++++++.>+++++++++++.+[->++++<]>-...++[->+++<]>+.++[--->++<]>.+[--->+
+<]>+.....+[----->+<]>.[---->+++<]>.+[->+++<]>+.>+++++++++++.--[--->++++<]>...>++++
+++++..-[->+++++<]>.[--->++<]>++.>-[--->+<]>--.[----->+++<]>.[--->+<]>---.-.+[--
-->+<]>+++.---[->+++<]>.------------.---.--[--->+<]>-.--[->+++++<]>--.[->+++<]>-.
++++++++++.+++++++++.++[->+++<]>.--[--->+<]>-.+++++[->+++<]>.---------.[--->+<]>
--.---[->++++<]>.------------.---.--[--->+<]>-.++[->+++<]>.+++.+++++++++.+.+.[---
->+<]>+++.+[->+++<]>++.+++++++..[++>---<]>--.----[->++++<]>.-----.[-->+<]>-----.
++[-->+++<]>.-----.>++++++++++.-[->++++<]>.[--->++<]>++.[->+++<]>++.[->+++<]>-----.++[--->+
+<]>.+[--->+<]>+.....+[-----><]>.[---->+++<]>.+[->+++<]>+.+++.-[->++++++<]>.[-->
+<]>+++.+++.+[--->+<]>-.---[->+++<]>---.+[----->+<]>+++.-----[->+++<]>-.--[-
--->+<]>--.---[->+++++<]>.------.[---->+++<]>-----.-------------.-----.---
-.--[--->+<]>-.[---->+<]>+++.---[->++++<]>-.---.------------.--.++++++.---.+++.---
---.[--->+<]>-.+++++[->+++<]>.+.------------.+++[->++++<]>++.--[---->+
<]>-.-----------.+++++.-.+++++.+[++>---<]>.++[--->++<]>.>-[--->+<]>-.[----->++++
<]>-.---.--[--->+<]>-.---[->+++++<]>-.+.+[->++++<]>++.--[--->+<]>---.++.[---->+<]>+
++.[->+++<]>+.+++++++++++++.-----------.-[--->+<]>-.+[->+++<]>++.+++++++.-------
---.-[--->+<]>-.+++++[---->+<]>.+[->+++<]>-.[->+++<]>+.-[->+++<]>.++[---
>++<]>.+++.+.[------->++<]>.[->+++<]>+.--[--->+<]>---.-------------.--[--->+<]>-.
.-[--->+<]>-.+++++.-----------.+++++.------.---.--[--->+<]>-.+++[->+++<]>.-.-[--->
+<]>-.[->+++<]>++.[--->+<]>+++.-[----->+<]>++.[->+++<]>.-----.+++++.[->+++<]>.[->+
++<]>+.+++++++++++++.-----------.-[--->+<]>-.[->+++<]>.+++.-----.>+++++++++++
+++.--[->+++++<]>-..---.[-->++++++<]>-.+[->+++<]>.++++.-----------.++++.----.-[--->
+<]>++.[->+++++<]>-.--[--->+<]>-.-----------.++++++.-.-[->+++++<]>-.>-[--->+<]>-.
.-[----->+++<]>.--.+++++.+++++++.-----.---[->+++<]>.+[->+++<]>+.[---->+<]>----.>+++
+++++.++[++++>---<]>.+[--->+<]>.-[->++++++<]>-.+[->+++<]>.---[----->+<]>.-.+++[
++++<]>++.+++++++.+++++.---------.-[--->+<]>--.+[->+++<]>+.+++++++++.+++[-----><]
>.-------------.---[->++++<]>.---------------.+++++++++++++.--------------.--[--->
+<]>-.[->++++<]>+.--[->+++<]>.-.--------------.--[--->+<]>-.[---->+<]>+++.[----->
++<]>+.--[--->+<]>-..+++[->+++<]>.+++++++++++++.-----.+++++.+[----->+<]>+++.[->+++<
]>+.+++++++++++++.-----------.-[--->+<]>-.---[->+++++<]>.---.------------.------.++++++
++.+++++++++.------.--[--->+<]>-.[->++++<]>-.[->+++++<]>-.------------.--[--->+<]>-
.+[->+++<]>.++++++++++++.-----------.-.--[--->+<]>-.+[----->+<]>.++.+++.----------
----.--[--->+<]>-.+[->+++<]>++.+.+++.------.------.+++++++++++.++++++.[++>---
<]>.++[--->+<]>.+++[->+++<]>.+[--->+<]>++.+++.[-->+++++<]>+++.+[->+++<]>++.[--->+
<]>+.--[->+++<]>-.-----------.+++.----.-------.-[->+++<]>.---[->+++<]>.
+<]>.--------------.---.+++++++++++++.--------------.--[--->+<]>-.[->+++<]>+.--[--->
+<]>---.-------------.--[--->+<]>-.---[->++++<]>.---.------------.--.++++++.---.+
++.+.[----->++<]>.+[->++++<]>.+++++++++++++.-----------.+.--[--->+<]>-.[--->++
++<]>.[----->++<]>+.--[--->+<]>--..+++[->+++<]>.+++++++++++++.-----.+++++.+[----->+<
]>+++.---[->+++++<]>.------.[--->+<]>-----.+++++[->+++<]>.+.++++.-----------.++++.-
---.-[--->+<]>++.---[->+++<]>.--[--->+<]>-.---[->++++<]>.------------.----.--[--->
+<]>-.+[--->++<]>.++.++++++++.[------->++<]>.+++++.-------.--[--->+<]>-.+++++[->+++
<]>.+++.[-->++++++<]>+++.+[->+++<]>.+++++++++++++.+.++++++++++.[->++++<]>--.+++++.---
----.-[--->+<]>--.+++++[->+++<]>.----------.[--->+<]>--.--[->++++<]>--.[->+++<]>-.
++++++++++++.++++++++++.++[->+++<]>.[--->+<]>-----.+[++>---<]>.>++++++++++.+[--->++++
+<]>.+[--->+<]>+++.-.++++++.--.---.---.[++>---<]>--.>-[--->+<]>--.[--->+<]>+++.--.+
++.+[->+++<]>+.-[--->+<]>--.+.---.-------------.[--->+<]>----.>+++++++++++..-[->++
                        -[----->+<]>--..
```

```
++<]>-..---.++++[->++<]>+.[->+++++<]>.+++.----.-------.++++++++.--------.++++++++
+.++++++.-----------.+++++.-------.-[--->+<]>--.++++[->++<]>+.---.[->+<]>---.>-[
--->+<]>--.[--->+<]>+++.+[->+++<]>++.--[--->+<]>-.+++[->+++<]>.++++++++.--------.
+++++++++.++++++.-.->+++++++++..>-[--->+<]>--.+[---->++++<]>.+++++.-----------.+
+.--[--->+<]>-.+[->+++<]>.---[----->+<]>-.+++[->+++<]>++.++++++++.+++++.--------.-
[--->+<]>--.+[->+++<]>+.+++++++.-[++>---<]>+.+[->+++<]>+.+++++++++.----------.
[--->+<]>----.-----.[++>---<]>++.[->+++<]>-.[---->+<]>+++.-[--->++<]>--.-------.+
[--->+<]>.+[->+++<]>.--[--->+<]>-.+[->+++<]>+.+++++.+++++++++.-------------.--.-[
--->+<]>--.[----->+<]>+++.+[->+++<]>.+++++++++++++.-.----------.+++++.+++++++++++.-
----------.+++++++.-.-------------.+++++++++++.[++>---<]>--.[->+++<]>++.[--->+<]>-
---.+++[->+++<]>++.+++++++++++++.-----------.+++++.+.+++++.-------.---[->+++<]>.-
-----------.++[--->++<]>.+++..+.+++.+[---->+<]>+++.[->+++<]>+.--[--->+<]>---.----
---------.--[--->+<]>-.---[->++++<]>+.--.++++[->+++<]>.-.-[--->+<]>-.---[->++++<]
>.-----.[--->+<]>-----.-[--->++<]>-.++++.+++.-----.--------.+++++++.---------.+++++
++++.++++++.[---->+<]>+++.++++[->++<]>+.----.[-->+<]>---.---[->++++<]>-.+.+[->+++<
]>++.--[--->+<]>-.+++[->+++<]>.+++++++++.--------.+++++++++.++++++.-.+[++>---<]>.>
+++++++++.--[->++++<]>-..---.[->+++++<]>--.-[--->+<]>.-.[----->++<]>+.+[->+++<
<]>-.[-->+++<]>-.[--->+<]>----.+.--.+++.+[->+++<]>+.-[--->+<]>--.----------.[->+
+++++<]>.+[->+++<]>.--[--->+<]>-.+++[->+++<]>.--[--->+<]>.+++.++++++++.+[----->+<]>
++.+[->+++<]>+.+[--->+<]>+++.-.++++++.--.---.---.>+++++++++..+[->++++++<]>+.+[---
>+<]>+++.+.++++++++.-[----->+<]>++.---[->++++<]>.------------.---.--[--->+<]>-.-[
--->++<]>-.+++++.++.+++++.-.[----->+<]>+++.--[->+++++<]>--.[->++++<]>-.++++++++++.+
++++++++.++[->+++<]>.--[--->+<]>-.++[->+++<]>.++++++++++.+++.[-->+++++<]>+++.+[->+
++<]>+.++++++++.--.+++.[----->++<]>-.++[->+++<]>---.---------.+++++++++.----.
---->+<]>----.+.--.+++.+[----->+<]>+.-[--->+<]>--.-----------.[->++++++<]>.+++++++
+++.--------.-[--->+<]>--.+[->+++<]>++.+++++++++++++.-----------.[++>---<]>--.--[->+++++<]>-
-.[->+++<]>-.++++++++++.+++.----------.---.--[--->+<]>-.-[--->++<]>-.+++++.++.+++
++.-.[----->+<]>+++.++.+++++++++.-[----->+<]>++.--[->++++<]>+.--.++++[->+++<]>.+[-
--->+<]>+++.+.++++++++.-[----->+<]>++.--[->++++<]>+.--.++++[->+++<]>.-.-[--->+<]>
-.+++[->+++<]>.--[--->+<]>-.+++[->+++<]>.----.[-->+++++<]>+++.+[->+++<]>+.+[-->+
+<]>+.+[-----<]>+..[--->++<]>++.+.--[->++++<]>+.+[->+++<]>++.[--->++<]>.[-->+++
+<]>.+[->+++<]>+.+[----->+<]>.[--->++<]>+.-[->+<]>.....[->+++<]>+.++[--->++<]>.
[-->++++<]>.[--->++<]>..[-->+++<]>--.-[--->+<]>.[->++++<]>.,..[-->+++<]>-....
[--->++<]>.+++++++++++.--[----->++<]>.[-->+++++<]>.[->++++++<]>+.++.>
-[--->+<]>---.+[----->++++<]>.--.++.+++++.[->+++++++<]>.+[->+++<]>.[--->+<]>---.+[-
--->+<]>+++.---[->++++<]>.-------------.---.--[--->+<]>-.-[--->++<]>-.+++++.++.+++
++.-.[----->+<]>+++.-[->+++++<]>--.[->++++<]>-.+++++++++++.++++++++++.++[->+++<]>.--
[->+++<]>-.[->+++<]>+.+++++++++++++.-----------.-[--->+<]>++.+[->+++<]>.+++++++++++++
+.+.-------.----.[--->+<]>----.+[----->+<]>+++.-[--->+<]>-.+++++++++++++.[--->+<]>
+++.++[->+++<]>.-----.>+++++++++.-[->+++++<]>.[--->++<]>++.++++[->++<]>+.>-
-[--->+<]>.[-->+<]>+.+.+++++.[++>---<]>--.------------.---[->+++<]>.-[--->++
++<]>.-----------.+.--.+++.+[->+++<]>+.-[--->+<]>--.------------.[->++++++<]>.+[->+++<]>
[->+++<]>.++.+++++++..[++>---<]>--.[->+++<]>++.+++.--.+++++++++++++.--.--------.[-
--->+<]>----.+[----->+<]>+++.---[->+++<]>.-------------.----.--[--->+<]>-.-[--->++<]
>-.+++++.++.+++++.-.[----->+<]>+++.--[->+++++<]>--.[->++++<]>-.+++++++++++.+++++++++
++++.----------.-[--->+<]>.---[->+++<]>.-------------.-[--->+<]>++.+++++++++++
+<]>-.++++[->+++<]>.--.++++++++++++++.-.-----------.-[--->+<]>-.+[->+++<]>.++.+++++++
+..[++>---<]>--.[->+++<]>++.+++.--.+++++++++++++.--.---------.[--->+<]>----.+[---->
+<]>+++.++[->+++<]>.-----.>+++++++++.-[->+++++<]>.[--->++<]>++.++++[->++<]>+.>-
-[--->+<]>.[-->+<]>+.+.+++++.[++>---<]>--.------------.---[->+++<]>.+++++++++++.+
++<]>.------------.---.--[--->+<]>-.++[->+++<]>.+++.++++++++++.+.+.[----->+<]>+++.+
[->+++<]>.++.+++++++..[++>---<]>--.[->+++<]>++.+++.--.+++++++++++++.--.---------.[-
--->+<]>----.+[----->+<]>+++.---[->+++<]>.-------------.----.--[--->+<]>-.-[--->++<]
>-.+++++.++.+++++.-.[----->+<]>+++.--[->+++++<]>--.[->++++<]>-.+++++++++++.+++++++++
.++[->+++<]>-.>+++++++++..-[->+++<]>-.+++++++++++++..-[->+++++<]>-....-++[->+++<]>-.[-
--->+<]>----.+.--.+++.+[->+++<]>+.-[--->+<]>--.------------.[->++++++<]>.+[->+++<]>
```

-[----->+<]>--.+.

```
.--[--->+<]>-.+++[->++[<]>.--[--->+<]>.+++.++++++++.+[---->+<]>++.+[->++<]>+.+[---
>+<]>+++.-.++++++.--.---.---.>+++++++++++.+[->+++++<]>++.++[-->+++<]>.++++++++++.
-----------.--.-[--->+<]>--.--------.-[--->+<]>.-[---->+<]>++.+++++[->+++<]>.+.
-----------.+++++++++++.+++[->+++<]>++.--[--->+<]>-.+++[->+++<]>.[--->+<]>----.
+[---->+<]>+++.+++++[->+++<]>.-.-[->++++<]>-.---[->++++<]>.------------.---.--[-
-->+<]>-.-[--->++<]>-.+++++.++.+++++.-.[---->+<]>+++.--[---->+++++<]>--.[->+++<]>.++
++++++++.++++++++.++[->+++<]>.-[->+++<]>.------------.+[----->+<]>.++.---------
--.+++++.---.-[--->+<]>++.[->+++<]>--.+++++.--------.-[--->+<]>--.-[--->+<]>-.+++
++++++++.[++>---<]>.>++++++++++.--[--->+<]>...++.[--->+<]>----.+++[->+++<]>++
.++++++++.+++++.---------.--[--->+<]>-.+[->+++<]>+.++++++++.>++++++++++.[->++++<
]>++.+[--->++<]>+.+++.[->+++<]>-.+[-->+<]>.--[-----><]>.+.-.[->+++++<]>.++.-.....+.
[->++<]>-.++[--->++<]>.[->+++<]>.[--->++<]>.[->+++++++++<]>.[--------->+<]>.[->+
++++++++<]>.[->+<]>-.[->+<]>.[--->++<]>.[->+++++<]>-...-[--->++++<]>-..[->+
++<]>--.-[--->+<]>.+[->++<]>+.-[-->+<]>.[->++<]>+..>+++++++++.--[--->++++<]>...>+
+++++++++.--[->+++++<]>.[--->++<]>++.++[->++<]>.++[-->+++<]>.++++++++++.----------
---.--.-[--->+<]>--.----------.-[--->+<]>.-[---->+<]>++.---[->++++<]>-.++.+[->+++<]
>.[--->+<]>--.--.+++[->+++<]>++.++.-[---->+<]>--.-.+[----->+<]>+++.++[->+++<]>.++++
++++++++.---.--.[->+++++<]>-.---[->+++<]>.------------.---.--[--->+<]>-.-[--->++
<]>-.+++++.++.+++++.-.[---->+<]>+++.--[->+++++<]>--.[->+++<]>-.+++++++++++.++++++
++.++[->+++<]>.--[--->+<]>-.++[->+++<]>.++++++++++.+++.[-->++++++<]>+++.+[->+++<]>.
++++++++++.-.----------.+++++.++++++++++++.-----------.+++++++++++.-.-[->+++++<]>-.+[
->+++<]>.+++++.---.--.+++++++++.--.+++++.-------.--[->+++<]>-.>+++++++++++.-[->++++
+<]>.[--->++<]>++.++++[->++<]>+.>--[----->+<]>.[--->+<]>--.---[->++++<]>--.
[->+++<]>-.++++++++++.+++++++++.++[->+++<]>.--[--->+<]>-.[->+++<]>++.--[->+++<]>--.
.+[----->+<]>+++.-----[->+<]>-.--[--->++<]>--.++++++++++.-[--->++++++<]>.>-[--->+<]>
--.--[->++++<]>-.+++++++.--[->++++<]>.++[->++<]>+.++++++++++.+++.+[-->+<]>.+++.----
---------.---[->++++<]>.------------.---.--.++[->+++<]>.++++++++++.+.
+.[---->+<]>+++.+[->+++<]>.++.+++++++.+.[++>---<]>--.[->+++<]>++.+++.--.++++++++++
++.--.---------.[--->+<]>-----.+[----->+<]>+++.++[-->+++<]>.++++++++.+[->+++<]>++.-[-
-->++<]>-.---.[--->+<]>--.+[----->+<]>+.+.++++++.[++>---<]>--.------------.---[->+
+++<]>.++++++++.---.---.-[--->+<]>.+++[->+++<]>.+++.++++++++.+.[---->+<]>+++.
+[->+++<]>.++.+++++++.[++>---<]>--.+[->+++<]>+.+++++++++++.----------.[--->+<]>-
---.+[----->+<]>+++.+[----->+<]>+.+.+++++.[---->+<]>+++.[->+++<]>++.+++.--.++++++++
+++++.--.----------.--[--->+<]>-.++[->+++<]>.------.++[--->++<]>.++++[->+++<]>+.+[--
->+<]>.-[--->++++<]>-.---[->++++<]>.---------------.+.+++++++++.+[->+++<]>+++.+[->+
++<]>.--.--[--->+<]>--.++++[->+++<]>.-[--->++<]>.------------.---[->+++++<]>.------
------.---.--[--->+<]>-.-[--->++<]>-.+++++.++.+++++.-.[---->+<]>+++.--[->+++++<]>-
-.[->+++<]>-.+++++++++++.++++++++.++[->+++<]>.--[--->+<]>-.++[->+++<]>.++++++++++
++.+[----->+<]>+++.+[----->+<]>+.+.+++++.[---->+<]>+++.[--->++<]>.++.----------
----.[--->+<]>----.++++[->+++<]>.++++++++++++++.++++.+[->+++<]>.-.-[->+++<]>++.>+++
++++++..-[->++++<]>-.----.[-->+++++<]>--.>--[----->+<]>.[--->+<]>----.+.+++[->+
++<]>++.-.-[--->+<]>-.++++++[->++<]>.[->++<]>+.++++.+++++++++++.[------>+<]>.
+[--->+<]>.+.+++.+[----->+<]>.+[->+++<]>.--.++++++++++++.-[->+++++<]>-.[->++
<]>++.+++.--[--->+<]>-.+[----->+<]>+.----------.[--->+<]>----.+.+++[->+++<]>.-.-[-
-->+<]>-.---[->++++<]>.-----.[--->+<]>-----.[->+++<]>+.++++++++++++.[--->+<]>-.-
[----->+<]>+.+[->+++<]>-.+.+++++++++++.++++.-----------.---[->++++<]>-.++[--->++<]>
].>-[--->+<]>-.[---->+++++<]>-.---.[--->++]>++.-[---->+<]>++.[->+++<]>+.--[--->+
<]>---.-----------.--[--->+<]>-.---[->++++<]>+.--.++++[->+++<]>.-.-[--->+<]>-.-
--[->++++<]>.-----.[--->+<]>>-.-[--->++<]>-.++++.+++.----.--------.++++++++++.---
-----.+++++++++.++++++.[---->+<]>+++.+[->+++<]>.++++++++++++.--.+++.-----.--------.
[--->+<]>+.[----->+<]>++.+[->+++<]>.+++++++++++++.-.-----------.+++++.++++++++++++.--
-----------.++++++.-.+++++.+[---->+<]>+++.[->+++<]>+.+++++++++++++++.-----------.-[---
>+<]>-.---[----->+<]>.------------.+++++++++++.-----------.---[->+++<]>-.>-----
----.++++++++++++.-----------.[->++++++<]>.+[->+++<]>.--[--->+<]>-.[-->++++++<]>.
++.---.------------.++.[--->+<]>----..----------.+++++.-------.--[->+++<]>-.>+++++
+++++..-[->+++++<]>...>+++++++++++..-[->++++<]>-.---.-----[->+++<]>.---------.++[--
->+<]>.[--->++<]>.[--->+<]>++.-[----->+<]>.++++.+++++++++.+++[->+++<]>++.+++++++++++
++++.,----.+++++.--------.-[--->+<]>--.++[->+++<]>+.-[----->+<]>+++++.-[->+++<]>.+++
++++++++++.++++[->+++<]>+.++++++.+++++++++++.++++[->+++<]>.[--->+<]>----.>+++++++++
<]>++.--[->+++++<]>.[--->++<]>.[--->+<]>++.---.---------.++++++++++.+++[->+++
<]>-.[--->+++++<]>-.----.+++++.-.[---->+<]>+++.--[--->+<]>-.[->+++++++<]>.++++++.---.[-
-[-->++++<]>.-.----.+++++.-.[---->+<]>+++.--[--->+<]>-.[->++++++<]>.+++++.----.[-
->++++++<]>+++.[-->+++++<]>--.[----->+++<]>-.++++++++++++.--------.>+++++++++++..>-

                    -[----->+<]>--.++.
```

```
[--->+<]>-.-[--->+<]>+.+++++++.-[---->+<]>++.--[->++++<]>-.-----.---------.++++++
+++++.-----------.+++++.--------.-[---->+<]>--.[->+++<]>+.-[->++++<]>.+[->+++<]>.---[
----->+<]>-.+++[->+++<]>++.++++++++.+++++.--------.-[--->+<]>--.+[->+++<]>+.+++++
+++.-[++>---<]>+.[-->++++++++<]>.++.---.--------.+++++++++++.+++[->+++<]>++.++++++
++++++.[->+++++<]>-.---[->++++<]>.-------------.--------.--[--->+<]>-.[---->+<]>+++
.+++++[->+++<]>.++++++.-.-----.+++++.-.+[---->+<]>+++.--[->++++<]>+.----------.+
+++++.---.[-->+++++<]>+++.+++++[->+++<]>.+++++++++.---------.-[->+++++<]>-.+[-----
>+<]>+.-------------.+++++++++++++.--------.[->+++<]>-.>+++++++++++..-[->+++++<]>-..
---.[--->+++++<]>.[--->+<]>++.---.---------.+++++++++++.+++[->+++<]>++.+++++++++++
+<]>.-------------.--------.--[--->+<]>-.[---->+<]>+++.+++++[->+++<]>.++++++.-.----
.+++++.-.-.+[---->+<]>+++.[->+++<]>+.++++++++++++..[++>---<]>--.[-->+++++++<]>.++.
---------.+++++.+++++.+[->+++<]>++.+.++++++++++.-------.--[--->+<]>-.[->+++<]>+.>
-[--->+<]>--.--[->++++<]>-.++++++..-[->++++<]>.+[->+++<]>.+++++.-------.--[--->+<
]>---.+++[->+++<]>++.++.-[--->+<]>--.+++[->+++<]>.+++++++++++++.+.+[---->+<]>+++.
-[--->+<]>.+++++.-[->+++++<]>.++++.-------------.+++.--------------.+.+++++++++++++
+.++[++>---<]>.>++++++++++..-[->++++++<]>...>+++++++++++..-[->+++++<]>-.---.----[->+
+<]>-.----------.++[--->++<]>.[->+++<]>+.-[++++>---<]>.-----.---.-----.--.--[--->+
<]>-.-----------.++++++.-.+++++.+[---->+<]>+++.+++++[->+++<]>.----------.[--->+<]>
--.+[->+++<]>.---[----->+<]>-.+++[->+++<]>++.++++++++++.+++++.--------.-[--->+<]>--.
+[->+++<]>+.++++++++.-[++>---<]>+.[-->+++++++<]>.[--->+<]>++.---.--------.++++++++++
++.+++[->+++<]>++.+++++++++++++..----.+++++.--------.>+++++++++++..-[->+++++<]>-..---
.>-[--->+<]>-.-[----->+<]>--.--.+++++.++++++.------.+++++.++++.++[--->++<]>.[--
>+<]>----.+[---->+<]>+++.++.-[--->+<]>--.+++[->+++<]>.+++++++++++.[->++++++<]>+.++[-
----->+<]>+.-------------.+++.--------.+++++.+++++.-------.-[--->+<]>--.++++++[->++
<]>.[------>+<]>-.--[--->+<]>---.------------.---.--[--->+<]>-.[-->++++++<]>.[--->+<
]>++.---.----------------.+++[->+++<]>++.++++++++++++.+++++++.>+++++++++++..-[-
>+++++<]>.[--->+++<]>++.+++++++++++..---[->+++<]>-.[--->+<]>++.[-->+++<]>+.--[--->+
>+<]>-.-.----------.--[--->+<]>---.----------.-[--->+<]>++.[->++++++<]>--.--[---
>+<]>-.-.-----------.++++++.-.+[---->+<]>+++.--.[--->+++++<]>--.[-->+++<]>--.[->+++<]>.
++[--->++<]>.--------.---.--[--->+<]>-.+[->+++<]>.++++++++++++.------------.+.--[--->+
+<]>-.+++++.++++++.-----.[--->+<]>-----.---[->++++<]>-.------.-------------.++++++
+++++.-[++>---<]>--.[----->++<]>.++++[->++++<]>.--.-[--->+<]>-.------------.++++
++.-.+++++.+[---->+<]>+++.---[->++++<]>.------.[--->+<]>-----.[--->+<]>++.+[->++++<]>++.
++.------.--------.+++++++++++++.-----------.++.--[--->+<]>-.---[----->++<]>.-----
--------.[--->+<]>--.--.++[->+++<]>++.+.++++++++.+++.---.+++++++++++.+++++.-----[+
+>---<]>.>+++++++++++.-[->+++++<]>.[--->+<]>+++.++++++++++.++[->+++<]>+.+[->++<
]>+++.--.---------.+++++++++.+++++.-.-[++>---<]>-.--[-->+++<]>--.[--->+<]>+++.>-
[--->+<]>--.+[---->+++++<]>.+++++.-----------.++.--[---->+<]>-.+[->+++<]>.++++++++++
++++.--.--------.+++++++++++.++++++.-.+[---->+<]>+++.[->+++<]>+.--[--->+<]>---.---
----------.--[--->+<]>-.[->+++++++<]>.-.++++.--[--->+<]>-.++++.[---->+<]>+++.+++++
---.--[--->+<]>-.-[--->++<]>-.+++++.-[--->++++<]>-.+[->+++<]>.---[----->+<]>-.+++[-
>+++<]>++.++++++++.+++++.--------.-[--->+<]>--.+[->+++<]>+.++++++++.-[++>---<]>+.
]>.-------------.-----[->++++<]>+.--.++++[->++++<]>.--[--->+<]>-.---[->++++<]>.------
------.----.++++++++.+++.[------->++<]>.---[->++++<]>+.-------.------------.+.++++++++++++
+.+.+.+[->+++<]>++.++++++++++++++.------------.-[--->+<]>-.---[->++++<]>.------------
-.---.--[--->+<]>-.[--->++<]>.++++++++++++.------------.+.--[--->+<]>-.+++++++++++..
-[->++++<]>-.,---.++[->+++<]>.[-->+++<]>-.---.---[->+++<]>.++[->++++<]>++.++.+++++.-
------.-[--->+<]>--.++++++[->+++<]>+.>--[----->+<]>-.[--->+<]>---.------------.+++
++++.-----------.--[--->+<]>---.>+++++++++++..-[->++++++<]>.[--->+<]>++.+++++++++++
.---[->+++<]>-.>--[--->+<]>-.+++++++++.++.++.+++++++.-[----->++<]>.>+.[-->++++<]>
.++++[->++++<]>+.++++++++++.++.[->+++<]>-.+++++++++++++.---.-[--->+<]>++.[->++++<
]>-.--[--->+<]>-.------------.++++++.-.+[->+++++<]>-..--[-->+++<]>--.[--->+<]>+++.>
-[--->+<]>.+[--->+<]>+.++++[->++++<]>.--[--->+<]>-.---[->++++<]>.-----.---.++++++
+.+.+++++.+++.--[->++++<]>.-----------.---------.--[--->+<]>-.[----->+<]>++.+[
->++++<]>+.+++++.+++++++++++.---.----.-----------.+[--->+<]>+++.-[--->+<]>++.---[-
>++++<]>.------------.---.--[--->+<]>-.---[->++++<]>-.+.+[->+++<]>++.--[--->+<]>-

                            -[----->+<]>--.+++.
```

```
.+++[->+++<]>.--[--->+<]>-.+++++[->+++<]>.----------.[--->+<]>--.+[----->+<]>.----
----.+++++++++.++.+++.+++++++.-----[++>---<]>.+++++++++++.-[->+++++<]>.[--->++<]>+
+.+++++++++++..[->++<]>-.[--->+<]>+++.+++[->+++<]>.+++++++++++.[------->++<]>.++[-
>++<]>+.-[----->+<]>++++.-[->+++<]>.--.-[--->+<]>--.-.-----------.++++++.-.+[->+++
++<]>-..--[-->+++<]>--.[-->+<]>+++.>-[--->+<]>.+[--->+<]>+.++++[->+++<]>.--[--->+
<]>-.[->+++<]>+.+++++++++++.-[->+++++<]>-.-[--->++<]>-.+++++.++++++.+++[->+++<]
>.++++++++++++.--.++.-------------.[--->+<]>---.+++[->+++<]>.+++++++++++.[-->+
++++<]>+++.---[->+++++<]>.------.[--->+<]>------.+[->+++<]>++.[--->+<]>+.-[->+++<]>.
--.-[--->+<]>-.-.+++[->+++<]>.--[--->+<]>-.[->+++<]>+.++++++++++.-----------.-[
--->+<]>-.--[->++++<]>--.+[->+++<]>.+++++++++++.----------.---.-[--->+<]>++.-[--
-->+<]>++.---[->+++++<]>.-------------.---.--[--->+<]>-.+[->+++<]>.++++++++++++.---
---------.+.--[--->+<]>-.++[->++<]>.---.+++++.----------.--[--->+<]>-.[->+++<]>++
.[--->+<]>+++.-[----->+<]>++.++[--->++<]>.---.+++++.---------.[->+++<]>-.>+++++++++
++..-[->+++++<]>-..---.[-->+++++<]>.>--[--->+<]>-.+++++++++++.-----------.+++
+++++++.+++.-----.------------.++++++++++++++.-----------.++.--[--->+<]>-.[->++++++
<]>-.+[--->+<]>.++++.-----------.++++.----.-[--->+<]>++.[->++++++<]>-.--[--->+<]>-
.-----------.++++++.-.+[------->++<]>-.-[--->+<]>-..------.++++++.-.+[->++++++<]>-..-
-[-->+++<]>--.[-->+<]>+++.>-[--->+<]>---.+[-----> +++<]>.+++++++++.++.+++++++.+[->+
++<]>++.--[--->+<]>---.+++++++.-[----->+<]>++.++[--->++<]>.+++.+.+++.[----->+<]>+++
+.[->+++<]>+.+++++++++++.----------.-[--->+<]>-.-----[->+++<]>-.+++++[->+++<]>+.+[---
>+<]>+++.-.------------.++++++++++.++++++++++.--.----------.++++++.-.-[->+++++<]>-.[
->+++<]>+.+++++++++++++++.----------.-[--->+<]>.+++[->+++<]>.[++>-------<]>.-.+.---
.-----------.--[--->+<]>-.++++++[->+++<]>.-[->+++++<]>+.-----.--[--->+<]>+++.---
-.-----.+++++.-------->+++++++++++.+[->++++++<]>.---[----->+<]>-.+++[->+++<]>++.+
+++++++.+++++.---------.-[--->+<]>--.+[->+++<]>+.+++++++++.-[++>---<]>+.-[--->+<]>
-.+++++++++.+[----->+<]>+++.--[--->+<]>--.+[----->+<]>++++.[->+++<]>++.-[->+++<]>.------
---.[++>---<]>--.[->+++<]>+.--[--->+<]>--.+[----->+<]>+++.[->+++<]>+.-[->+++<]>.+[
----->+<]>.---------.----.+++++++++++++.+++++.+[----->+<]>+++.---[->++++<]>.------.[
--->+<]>-----.+[->+++<]>+.+..++++++++++++.-----------.+++++++++.-[->+++++<]>-.--[-
>+++<]>+.----------.++.+.+.+[->+++<]>++.+++++++++++++.----------.+++++.+++++.--------.-[
--->+<]>--.+++++[->+++<]>.----------.[--->+<]>--.[-->++++++<]>.++.---.----------.++
++++++++.+++[----->+++<]>++.----------.--[--->+<]>--.[->+++<]>.--[--->+<]>-.[-
>+++<]>--.-[--->++<]>-.++++++++++++.-.+[----->+<]>+++.+[->+++<]>++.[--->+<]>+.----.
--.-------------.+++++++.----------.--[-->+<]>-.---[->++++<]>-.-----------.++++.++
+.----.---.------.+++++++.++++++++++.+++++.-[--->++<]>-.---[->++++<]>.+++++++++++++
.----------.------.++++++.+++++++++++.------.+[-----> +++<]>++.++[--->++<]>.+[
->++<]>.-----[->++<]>-.-[----->+<]>++.+[----->+<]>.-------------.--[----->+<]>--.+.++
+[->+++<]>.+++++++++++++.---------.[->+++++<]>-.---[->++++<]>.+++[-
>+++<]>.--.+++++.-------.-----.++++++++++.++++.++[->+++<]>.[--->+<]>----.+[---->+<]>
+++.++[->+++<]>.++++++++++++.---.--.[->+++++<]>-.---[->++++<]>.------------.---.-
-[--->+<]>-.[->+++<]>++.-.--[--->+<]>--.---------.-----------.--[--->+<]>---.+[----->+<
]>++.---[->+++++<]>.------.[--->+<]>+.+++.--[--->+<]>.[->+++<]>-.+++++++++++++
+++++++++++++.-----------.++.-.-[--->+<]>-.++[--->++<]>.-------.[--->+<]>-.+[->+++<
]>.++++++++.++++++++.-[++>---<]>+.-------------.--[->+++<]>+.----------.++++++.-[--
```

```
-[----->+<]>--.++++.
```

-->+<]>+++.+[->+++<]>.--.+++++++++++.-[->+++++<]>-.[->+++<]>+.-[++>-----<]>..--
--.-[--->+<]>.-[---->++<]>++.---[->++++<]>.-------------.---.+++++++.[->+++++<]>-.
---[->++++<]>.-----.[--->+<]>-----.+++++[->+++<]>.+++++.-------------.---.+++++++
+++++.[-->+++++<]>+++.++[--->++<]>.------------.+++++++++++++.-------.--[--->+<]>-
-.[->+++<]>++.+++++++.---[->++++<]>-----.+[---->+<]>+++.[->+++<]>+.++++++++++++.---
-------.-[--->+<]>-.+[->+++<]>.+++++++++++++.-.------------.++.+++++++++++.++++.-.+
[---->+<]>+++.-[--->+<]>-.+++++.-[->+++++<]>-.+[->+++<]>.++++++++++++.--.+++.+++
++.-.+++[->+++<]>.+++++++++++++.[-->+++++<]>+++.---[->++++<]>-.+++[->+++<]>+.++++
++.----.++++++++.-----------.++.[->+++<]>-.++[--->++<]>.++++[->+++<]>+.[->+++<]>+++
.------.+++++.-------.-[--->+<]>--.++[->+++<]>.++++++++++.+++.+++++.-[->+++<]>-.--
[--->+<]>---.----------------.[->+++<]>.-------------.--[->++++<]>+.-----------.+++++
+.-[---->+<]>+++.+[->+++<]>.--.+++++++++++.-[->+++++<]>-.++[->+++<]>.-[--->+<]>
--.---.++.-------------.--.+++++++++++.+++++++++++++.+[-->+++++<]>+++.++++++++.
-------.-------.++++++++++++++.------------.++.--[--->+<]>-.--[->++++<]>+.----------.
+++++++.---.[-->+++++<]>+++.[-->++++++<]>.++.---.--------.+++++++++++.+++[->+++<]
>++.+++++++++++++..-----.+++++.-------.-[--->+<]>--.---[->++++<]>-.---------.--.+++.
.+++++++.+[---->+<]>+++.[->+++<]>++.[->+++<]>++.[->+++<]>+.[->+++<]>.++++++.
------.+++++++++++.-------.+++++++++++.-------.++.+++++.-------.-[--->+<]>--.--[->
++++<]>+.---------.++++++.---.+.++++[->+++<]>.+++++++.------.[--->+<]>--.--[->++
+++<]>-.+[->+++<]>+.+++++++++++++.-----------.--[--->+<]>--.+[----->+<]>.++.+++.----
--------.--[--->+<]>-.+[->+++<]>.+++++++++++++.--.+++.-------.[--->+<]>+.[-
---->+<]>++.[-->+++++++<]>.++.---.--------.+++++++++++++.+++[->+++<]>++.+++++++++
.++++++.+[---->+<]>+++.-[--->+<]>-.+++++.-[->+++++<]>-.+[->+++<]>.---[----->+<]>.
.+++[->+++<]>++.+++++++.+++++.-------.-[--->+<]>--.+[---->+<]>++.+++++++.-[++>--
-<]>+.+++++[->+++<]>.+++.[-->+++++<]>+++.++[--->++<]>.--------.-----.--[--->+<]>.
.----.-----.+++++.--------.-[--->+<]>--.+++++[->+++<]>.+++++.-------------.---.++++
++++++++.[-->+++++<]>+++.+[->+++<]>++.[--->+<]>----.----.+++++.+++[->+++<]>.++++
++++++++.------.-------.+[->+++<]>----.++[--->++<]>.+.-[->+++<]>.++..---------.+++++++++
.+++[->+++<]>++.+++++++++++++.----.+++++.-------.-[--->+<]>--.++[--->++<]>.-------
----.+++++++++++++.-------.--[--->+<]>--.[->+++<]>++.++++++.--.[--->+<]>----.+[++
>---<]>.

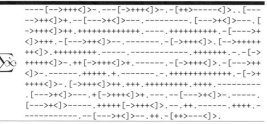

ISBN 978-4-87310-283-2
C0004 ¥250E
本体 250 円

THE DARKSIDE COMMUNICATION GROUP

Picardスキームの代数的構成

Main theorem

$$\mathrm{Pic}_{(X/S)(\text{ét})}(-)\colon (\mathrm{Sch}/S)^{op} \to (\mathrm{Set})$$

is representable.

ProjectiveX

暗黒通信団